the**airport**
serving the East Midlands for 40 years

the**airport**

serving the East Midlands for 40 years

words by

Bob Walker

designed and produced by

origination

Nottingham
East Midlands Airport

40YEARS
Nottingham East Midlands Airport
1965-2005

First published in Great Britain in 2005
by Nottingham East Midlands Airport
Castle Donington, Derby, East Midlands DE74 2SA

Paperback edition: ISBN-10 0-9552010-0-4
                   ISBN-13 978-0-9552010-0-4
Hardback edition: ISBN-10 0-9552010-1-2
                   ISBN-13 978-0-9552010-1-1

Designed and produced by Origination
St Peter's House, St Mary's Wharf, Mansfield Road, Derby DE1 3TP
Printed in the East Midlands, Great Britain.

We would like to thank the Derby Evening Telegraph, Leicester Mercury, Nottingham Evening Post and the many
individuals who have supplied their photographs for use.

Acknowledgements

THE 40-YEAR history of Nottingham East Midlands Airport is one that tells the story of people; those who had the vision and the talent to make the airport into the success story it is today, but also those who use the airport as passengers.

Throughout the writing of this book, I have been grateful for the help and guidance of many people who have taken time to share with me their recollections of the airport and to explain the more complex aspects of operating a busy international airport.

Without their help, this celebration of NEMA's 40-year history would have been a much greater challenge.

My thanks go especially to John Baddiley and Bill Blanchard at NEMA, both of whom assisted me with the more technical developments seen at the airport over the years. John's technical knowledge of the airport is unmatched whilst Bill, as he said himself, has aviation in his blood.

I would also like to thank the following members of staff from NEMA for their contributions: Penny Coates, Barry Thompson, John Froggatt, Colin Sorrell, Simon Whitby, Brian Conway, Dianne Letts and Mick Hodgkin.

I would also like to thank NEMA employees Jessica Dear, Ryan Martinez and Caroline Plant for their assistance with this project.

A number of past employees also assisted me. My thanks go to John Spooner, John Anscombe, Dave Fairweather, Sue Underwood, Owen Ward and Alan Webb.

Thanks also to David Gretton for allowing me to use his words about the early history of East Midlands Airport.

The following also contributed to this history of the airport: Sir Michael Bishop, Eileen Derrick, David Moores, Karen Smith, Monica Snowden, Noel Towler, Steve Gensler and Nick Walker.

A big thank you also goes to Derby-based design house Origination who created this superb book, and for their support throughout the writing process.

Finally, I would also like to pay tribute to Eric Dyer whose personality dominates the early part of the airport's story – **Bob Walker, November 2005**

Foreword | HRH Duke of Edinburgh

I AM DELIGHTED to have this opportunity to congratulate the management and staff of Nottingham East Midlands Airport on 40 highly successful years since I was invited to open it in 1965. It is very encouraging to know that there has been such a tremendous growth and development of all the services it offers to its burgeoning list of customers.

The author of this commemorative book provides a comprehensive overview of the process that turned a modest regional airfield into a thriving international airport. He gives the reader a fascinating insight into the hectic life of the airport from its inception to the present day through the eyes of the key people responsible for its development.

The story also reflects the breakneck speed with which the world's civil aviation business has evolved over the last half century.

Contents

Left:
A study in contrasts – a Lockheed Hercules freight aircraft which, in September 1967, became the largest plane ever to land at the airport, alongside one of the smallest machines to use it, a Nipper MK III.

Prologue

AS A BOY, I used to climb regularly to the top of Bardon Hill, the highest point in Leicestershire near Coalville, with a telescope strapped to my back.

I did not plan to gaze at the stars but to look across the 10 miles or so at the activity on the apron of the then East Midlands Airport.

To be fair, back in the early 1970s there was not too much activity to observe; a couple of holiday jets at best, but it was enough to conjure up dreams of far-off exotic destinations for a boy whose horizons were only just beginning to widen.

Through the eyepiece all I saw was glamour.

I was never a plane spotter. Although interested in new developments in the aviation world, I have never been able to reel off aircraft types; I have always been more interested in the excitement to be found in and around airport terminal buildings.

Even today, if I am at Nottingham East Midlands Airport, I will more often than not take a walk through the terminal building, browse in the bookshop, or take a cup of coffee. There is an excitement in the air, a look of expectation on people's faces, just a little sense of apprehension.

For me it all adds up to that one word – glamour.

And that is before you add in the planes, the pilots and the cabin crew.

But back in 1965 things were a little less glamorous.

Opposite page:
It's 1965 and an early view from the Air Traffic Control tower.

Left:
Air Traffic Control – 1988.

Below:
Aerial view from the south of the aircraft maintenance area in the late 1970s.

Chapter One | 1965-1969

ALAN WEBB recalls the day in 1965 that he came to see East Midlands Airport Director Eric Dyer about the role of Chief Fire Officer at the fledgling airport.

"It was a wet Saturday morning and Castle Donington village didn't look at its best when I stopped for a cup of tea. The airport looked like a building site. Mr Dyer told me to take a walk around and then come back for a chat.

"By the time I got back to his office I was wet and my shoes where muddy. It hadn't taken long to have a look around; at that time there was not that much to see."

That was 40 years ago and Mr Webb was one of the first senior figures recruited into Eric Dyer's team.

"I was told by someone from Birmingham that East Midlands Airport would do well to last six months. To be honest I thought that if that was the case at least I would get some knowledge and experience out of it."

Alan Webb retired in 1992 with an MBE for his services and 27 years of happy memories of working at the airport.

Having been in the RAF, Mr Webb would have been aware of some of the airfield's fascinating history.

Writing about the days before commercial operations, David Gretton states: "There has been flying activity on the site since World War One, but the story really began in the 1930s when the RAF was rapidly expanding to combat the German threat."

David goes on to explain how the first paved airstrip was laid down at Castle Donington airfield in 1942.

"Operational fighter squadrons naturally had priority but, following the Battle of Britain, the RAF's attentions were turned more to offensive operations – particularly the night bomber offensive.

"To cater for the expansion of Bomber Command a massive airfield construction programme began, and Operation Training Units (OTU's) were set up to provide crews with final training before a posting to the frontline.

"One of the new stations was at Wymeswold, a few miles north-east of Loughborough, which was opened on April 16th 1942 as part of 93 Group, Bomber Command.

"It was quickly realised that Wymeswold needed a relief landing ground to allow it to cope with its busy flying programme, so construction of a paved airfield began at Castle Donington.

"This became operational on 1st January 1943, when part of Wymeswold's resident unit, 28 OTU, moved in bringing with them Wellington I's and III's. In addition, Martinets and Masters were used by 28 OTU for target towing, and in some references Lysanders are also mentioned."

David picks up the story as D-Day approaches.

"In the period leading up to D-Day, crews from RAF Castle Donington operated special flights to drop propaganda leaflets to the patriots of occupied Europe.

"Shortly after the invasion, on June 11th 1944, it was decided to make RAF Castle Donington the centre for training the Pathfinder Force.

Opposite page:
An early view of the aircraft maintenance area at EMA. Part of the former RAF barracks can be seen at the top of this picture.

Following pages:
Construction of the taxiways – 1964.

1950

1950

Drawbacks of Burnaston aerodrome realised. East Midlands Airport Joint Committee formed to look for new site

Late 1950's

1951

Winston Churchill is re-elected as British Prime Minister aged 77

1955

Anthony Eden elected British Prime Minister

1957

British Prime Minister – Harold Macmillan 1957-1963

Soviet Union launches 'Sputnik' and starts the Space Race

1961

Berlin Wall erected

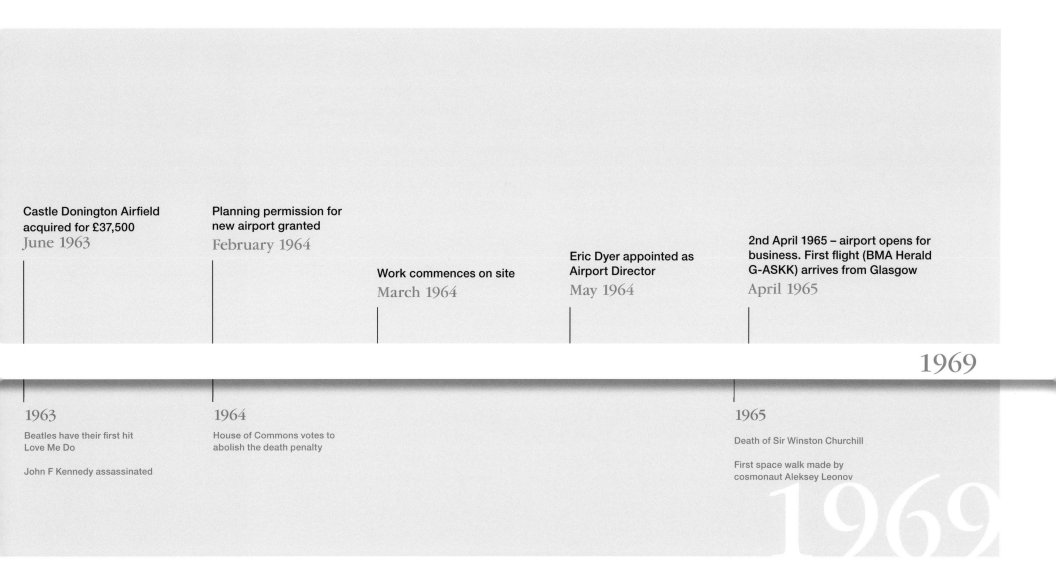

**Castle Donington Airfield
acquired for £37,500**
June 1963

**Planning permission for
new airport granted**
February 1964

Work commences on site
March 1964

**Eric Dyer appointed as
Airport Director**
May 1964

**2nd April 1965 – airport opens for
business. First flight (BMA Herald
G-ASKK) arrives from Glasgow**
April 1965

1969

1963

Beatles have their first hit
Love Me Do

John F Kennedy assassinated

1964

House of Commons votes to
abolish the death penalty

1965

Death of Sir Winston Churchill

First space walk made by
cosmonaut Aleksey Leonov

1969

"However, with the end of the war in Europe in sight, attention was drawn to the need for training additional transport crews who would be required for the Far East and the post-war period."

David records that on December 1st 1944 the airfield at Castle Donington consisted of three runways measuring 2,000 yards x 50 yards, 1,400 yards x 50 yards, and 1,100 yards x 50 yards.

"28 OTU officially disbanded on October 15th 1944 and was replaced by 108 OTU, which was formed on October 10th 1944 at Wymeswold with no fewer than 40 Dakotas. At that time, Castle Donington retained its satellite status.

"At the end of the war these transport aircraft were used to give the hard-worked ground crew 'Cook's Tours' of the bomb damage in Europe.

"With the general contraction of the armed forces that followed the end of the war, RAF Castle Donington was closed in September 1946."

Following the end of hostilities, civil flights from the East Midlands were recommenced by Derby Airways – who later became British Midland Airways – from the grass airfield at Burnaston, south-west of Derby city centre.

Burnaston, while it catered well for smaller passenger aircraft during the late 1940s and 1950s, was prone to waterlogging and came under increasing pressure as aircraft got larger to cope with the growing demand for overseas holidays.

After representations from Derby Airways, Derby Corporation discussed the future of flights from the region with Nottingham Corporation. Together they considered replacing Burnaston, now the site of the Toyota car factory, with a new civil airport that would be designed, built and financed by the local authorities.

David Gretton takes up the story: "Many sites were investigated, including Wymeswold. Eventually, the site of the old wartime Castle Donington airfield in Leicestershire was selected, close to the proposed extension of the M1 motorway.

Right:
Aerial shot of Castle Donington Airfield taken during World War Two.

Right:
Original artist's illustration of the
new East Midlands Airport.

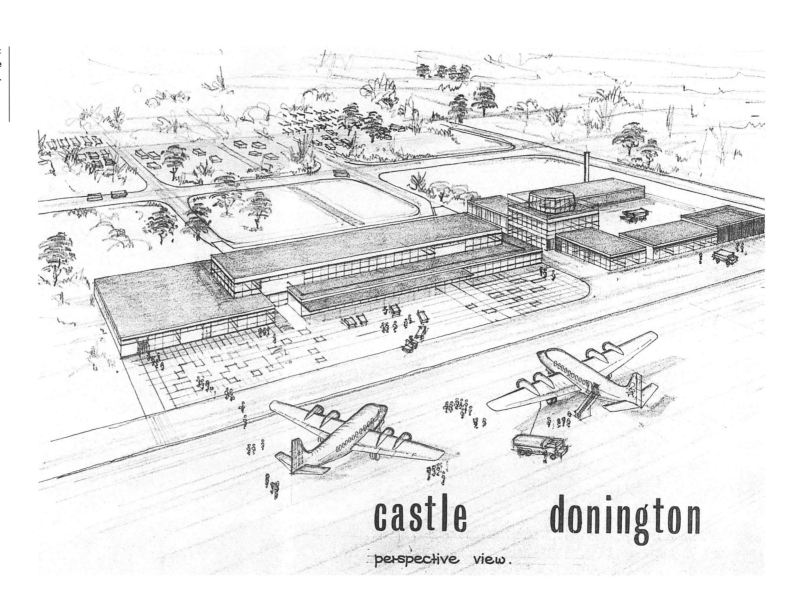

castle donington

perspective view.

"A joint committee of representatives from the county councils of Derbyshire, Leicestershire and Nottinghamshire and the city councils of Derby and Nottingham was set up to finance and run the new airport.

"In 1963 the Joint Airport Committee reached agreement to proceed with the construction, basing their decision on an estimated cost of £1.375 million for the initial venture. This sum was to be split between the authorities involved."

David records that the Ministry of Housing and Local Government approved the project and that the site was handed over to the main construction contractor, Richard Costain Ltd, on March 9th 1964.

"This company was responsible for clearing the site, breaking up the original runways – which had deteriorated to a point where they were not even suitable as a foundation for the new development – and for building the new runway.

"The runway was to be 5,850 feet long and 150 feet wide, with taxiways up to 60 feet wide. The new runway followed the line of the original main runway, whilst a grass strip of 2,900 feet on an alignment of 01/19 was additionally laid out for light aircraft," states David.

Richard Costain Ltd were also responsible for building approximately two miles of internal roads on the landside of the airport and for developing car parking facilities for about 850 vehicles.

Around this time the Joint Airport Committee appointed Eric Dyer as Airport Director.

Mr Dyer had been a pilot during World War Two and had extensive experience in airfield management, having held the post of Airport Director at both Southampton and Leavesden airports.

"Respect was the word you heard used about Mr Dyer," recalls Mick Hodgkin, who has worked at the airport since the 1970s and today is Facilities Supervisor Mechanical at Nottingham East Midlands Airport.

"He was firm but fair and people looked up to him for that.

"I suspect he also had a wicked sense of humour; I could never figure out if he was joking when he answered the phone with a brisk 'Dyer here' response," said Mick.

Temporary accommodation for Mr Dyer and his staff of 51 (today more than 6,500 people work on the site) was taken in Castle Donington while the administration block was constructed.

David Gretton continues: "The terminal building and all necessary service buildings were constructed by J Searson Ltd, mainly using the Consortium of Local Authorities Special Projects system (CLASP)."

Even when looking at the latest aerial photographs of NEMA it is easy to identify the first phase of the terminal construction.

NEMA Cargo Manager Bill Blanchard said:"One of the most fascinating aspects of the airport over the years has been how the terminal building has been adapted to meet the current needs.

Above:
An early image of the crew briefing room, showing Lanson tubes.

Right:
View of airport service buildings,
the terminal building and the apron – 1967.

Far right:
Queen Elizabeth the Queen Mother,
visiting East Midlands Airport on
9th November 1977.

Previous pages:
Landside departure concourse.

"The CLASP system was originally used in the construction of schools, which is one of the reasons why today there are so many pillars throughout the terminal building."

Construction work continued apace as the airport headed towards its planned opening date of 1st April 1965.

David Gretton states: "Construction was still going on at the last minute. In the haste a digger vehicle severed one of the main lighting cables, delaying by some hours the issue of the Ministry of Aviation Licence to operate as a civil airport.

"However, the problem was soon overcome and East Midlands Airport opened its doors, and its runway, to the air-travelling public the following day on April 2nd 1965."

Alan Webb also remembers having to use 'goosenecks'.

"A 'gooseneck' is like a watering can with a gooseneck spout, filled with paraffin. After the cable was severed, we used lighted goosenecks along the side of the runway until the power supply was restored."

By modern standards it was a rudimentary set-up, mirrored elsewhere in the airport's facilities.

John Baddiley, today NEMA's Airfield Engineering Supervisor, said: "The navigation aid equipment at the airport was very limited back in 1965.

"There was no instrument landing system or any other sophisticated navigation aids in use today.

"The very basic Decca 424 radar could be used for 'talkdown', but this was used only during very bad weather when pilots could not see enough out of the cockpit window to land using a visual approach.

"An air traffic controller sat in what was referred to as The Cupboard, a very small room beneath the old control tower, and gave verbal heading information via radio-telephone to pilots and literally talked them down to half a mile from the end of the runway.

"East Midlands Airport opened with a very basic runway, after which runway-approach and taxiway lighting was installed to aid operations during darkness.

Above:
Noel and Gwen's Wedding Day – 1965.

Previous pages:
**Runway and surrounding area
seen from the air.**

"Even so, the airport was not properly open for night-time operations until much later on."

But it was open!

Noel Towler was full of excitement as he made the journey from Alvaston in Derbyshire to the newly-opened East Midlands Airport.

It was his wedding day, April 3rd 1965, and he and his bride Gwen were set to embark on a short honeymoon flight to Jersey.

What sort of airport awaited them?

Mr Towler recalls: "Until shortly before the day, we were not sure whether we would be flying from Burnaston Airfield or the new East Midlands Airport.

"We got married at midday and were booked on the 5 o'clock flight to Jersey from the new airport.

"We drove up through Castle Donington, turning left at the Nags Head pub half way up the hill to head for the terminal building.

"I remember that my mother wouldn't come with us to the airport as she was unnerved by the thought of us getting on an airplane."

Mr Towler has returned to the airport many times since, and is very aware of just how passenger facilities in the terminal building have developed over the last 40 years.

"Back in 1965 departures and arrivals were under one roof, so all the passengers were in the same area.

"We were booked on what was referred to as the 'Honeymoon Special', as most people on the flight were off to Jersey on honeymoon. There were also 12 people celebrating their silver wedding anniversaries, having been married in 1940.

"Although I suspect there was a bit of nervousness, everyone appeared happy as we waited for the flight.

"We were all in it together and thought it was great fun. I had been in the Air Corps but my wife had never flown before. It was a real adventure."

Mr and Mrs Towler left on time but actually took almost 24 hours to get to Jersey.

Fog prevented them from landing in the Channel Islands and, being without passports, the passengers were not allowed to land in Dinard.

Instead, they spent the night at a plush hotel near Southampton before resuming their journey the following day.

Noel Towler was right to call it an adventure. But not just for passengers. There was a feeling amongst Eric Dyer's staff that they too were embarking on a journey that would be full of challenges.

John Baddiley takes up the story of the airport's technical limitations back in 1965: "We used a CE178 Cathode Ray Direction Finder (CRDF), made by Ecko of Southend.

"This picked up transmissions from aircraft, giving air traffic control the compass bearing to or from EMA.

"In effect, it was used as a 'homing' facility and had been developed during World War Two to guide bombers home after raids.

"If the aircraft flew along the bearing towards EMA that the CRDF was indicating, it would eventually arrive overhead.

Left:
A send-off for one of the twenty newly-wed couples who departed on the same flight as Noel and Gwen Towler - April 1965.

Below:
A postcard published by A.W. Bourne of Leicester, on behalf of British Midland, shows the Herald Aircraft and passengers in flight – Noel and Gwen Towler are circled.

"This would be signified when the bearing flipped by 180° as the aircraft began flying away, rather than towards, the airport.

"The CRDF bearing information was used with a stopwatch to enable accurate control of the rate of descent so that a primitive approach procedure could be flown. This allowed us to line up an aircraft with the end of the runway, which was especially useful when mist or cloud prevented pilots from flying visually."

The technical aids the pilots used were also rudimentary.

John Baddiley continued: "There was a Non-Directional Beacon (NDB) initially installed on the runway centreline near to the old Kegworth Railway Station. This device was made by Shorrocks of Blackburn and operated on similar principles to the CRDF. But it provided bearing information on a radio compass to the pilot, rather than to Air Traffic Control.

"The NDB transmitted a radio carrier wave on a frequency that was about halfway between the old 'long' and 'medium' wavebands.

"The Morse code identity CA was applied so that pilots could tune-in and positively identify the NDB. It became known as Charlie-Alpha (CA), derived from the original callsign of EMA, which was Castledon.

"Pilots could use this as a non-precision approach aid in bad weather.

"Derby Airways pilots, who had relocated to EMA from Derby's Burnaston Airfield, used procedures based on the Charlie-Alpha NDB to replace the Decca letdown procedures that had been in use since the 1950s.

"Following the move from Burnaston, Derby Airways rebranded themselves as British Midland Airways. For many years they were the only airline based at East Midlands Airport."

Looking back from our technologically advanced position now, these old systems have a Heath Robinson feel about them. But they allowed East Midlands Airport to take its first steps on the road that has led to the sophisticated commercial operation that we all know today.

Right:
The Passenger 'Check-in' Desks.
An exterior viewing balcony can be seen
through the upper windows with Airport
Administrative Offices located on the
first floor – 1967.

Left:
The Main Restaurant – Waitress Service.
Capable of seating approximately 60
people, catering for luncheons and
dinners – 1967.

Right:
Terminal building.

Far right:
Senator Edward Kennedy and his wife
at EMA in 1965 – the first of many VIPs
to sign the airport visitor book.

Eric Dyer had been tasked with having EMA up and working by April 1st 1965 with a construction period of just 13 months.

Mr Dyer brought an energy and vision to the project, earning respect that has endured across the decades.

For Karen Smith there is no doubt that, without his drive, the airport – if you will excuse the pun – would never have got off the ground.

She recalls: "I was working at the council offices in Castle Donington in 1965 when one day Eric Dyer came to see me.

"I had a big office to myself and he parked himself on the windowsill and started to talk about his plans for the airport.

"At first he put the fear of God into me, but then I started to listen and soon we were getting on like a house on fire. He had a vision for the airport. He had been presented with a big challenge and he was determined to succeed."

Eric Dyer had flown with 247 Squadron in World War Two and was in his mid-40s by the time he became the airport's first director.

"Eric may have had a few doubts about the project but he was going to make it work come hell or high water," said Mrs Smith.

"They couldn't have got anyone better for the job. He was firm but fair and generated fierce loyalty from his staff.

"There was not much he didn't know about the people who worked for him. He remembered the names of wives, husbands and children and always had a word for people – whatever their role. But he also knew how to use his power; it was just that he didn't need to demonstrate it all of the time."

Mick Hodgkin remembers one day when he was in the terminal building on a day off with his family.

"Mr Dyer came over and said he had a problem with the water system and asked whether I could fix it.

"I started to explain it was my day off but he reminded me of my responsibility to the airport and, sure enough, I fixed the system.

Above:
Fresh flowers flown in from the Channel Islands.

Left:
Inside the cockpit of a British Midland Airways Argonaut.

Following pages:
Aerial shot.

Right:
British Midland DC3 Cargo plane
being loaded.

Previous pages:
Terminal Apron, 12 acres of concrete.

"We all respected him. We used to have a laugh about his parking space between the terminal building and the old control tower. There was a gap there giving you a view through onto the airfield. We called it Dyer Straits.

"Don't get me wrong, it might have been a laugh at his expense but we had real respect for the man," he said.

Karen Smith recalled an encounter between Mr Dyer and someone he had dismissed some months earlier.

"The man came up to Eric and said 'Hello Mr Dyer. Do you remember me? You gave me the sack'.

"Eric replied 'Oh, jolly good'. Then they had a good chat about things. The man didn't bear a grudge."

She remembers Eric Dyer, who died in June 2004, as a man of great intelligence with a sharp sense of humour.

"For those who really got to know him, he was brilliant company, a good speaker," she said.

"But he was always very reserved about his achievements. I once told him that EMA was his airport, and always

would be. 'Thank-you for that' was his quiet reply."

The real focus in 1965 was on getting passenger operations under way. Cargo movements, which would later become such an important part of the airport's operations, grew initially by accident.

NEMA Cargo Manager Bill Blanchard said: "The Cargo 1 terminal was a small building on the edge of the apron and it was some time before the real potential of cargo operations was recognised."

David Gretton states: "Passenger numbers for the first year of operation came to 114,888, using 81 different types of aircraft. By contrast, 4.4 million people used NEMA in 2004.

"Despite setbacks due to the financial failure of several of the major operators from the airport in the early years, traffic increased steadily until 1968, the number of passengers for that year exceeding 250,000.

"The quantity of freight passing through the airport had been raised significantly and, for the first time,

British Midland operated all-freight aircraft on a number of routes."

By the end of the decade the terminal building was beginning to feel the strain. In April 1969, four years after operations began, the decision was taken to extend it, while also increasing the runway length to 7,480 feet, and widening the taxiways to 75 feet.

Fire Chief Alan Webb had by now realised that his job would last more than six months. And Eric Dyer had completed the first phase of his dream.

East Midlands Airport had lift-off!

Below:
Air freight aircraft were rarely seen, it was common practice for cargo to be transported on passenger aircraft.

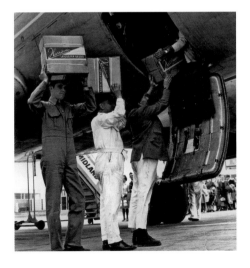

DLANDS AIRPORT

D ON 21ST JULY 1965

BY

OYAL HIGHNESS

Right:
His Royal Highness the Duke of Edinburgh
at Castle Donington Airport 21st July 1965.

Previous pages:
His Royal Highness the Duke of Edinburgh
unveils a plaque commemorating the
opening of the Airport.

Left:
His Royal Highness the Duke of Edinburgh takes in the view from the 'new' Air Traffic Control tower.

Chapter Two | 1970-1979

WRITING in the annual report of East Midlands Airport at the end of the 1970's, Councillor Walter Marshall, who was Chairman of the airport's management board, paid tribute to Eric Dyer and his management team.

Councillor Marshall said: "Without their contribution, the airport's success story would not be possible. They make the airport tick."

Eric Dyer would have understood and welcomed the praise but I believe he would have recognised that the airport's success was the result of the hard work of more people than just his management team.

Mr Dyer always looked after his airport workers and got the best out of them as a result.

John Anscombe, who worked as a member of the airport's duty crew for the 10 years between 1967 and 1977, recalled a time when he was experiencing problems at home.

"I was worried about the health of my wife and the welfare of my young family.

"One morning I got a call asking me to go to see Mr Dyer. My first thought was 'what's this all about?'

"I went into his office and he said 'Here's a whisky – drink it. You are going home to look after your family. Come back when things settle down'.

"Until everything was back to normal I used to go and sign my timesheet and my wages were paid as normal."

Mr Anscombe's role at the airport saw him involved in many facets of EMA's day-to-day operations.

Fire Chief Alan Webb explains: "It wasn't until the 1980s that I actually had a full-time fire service.

"Before then the airport's duty crew were also trained for fire service duties.

"They would also operate as baggage handlers, help with the arrival and departure of aircraft and carry out tasks within the terminal building."

He recalls: "We did a bit of everything really.

"When a plane arrived at the airport we would take the steps out to the aircraft along with the power unit.

"We'd also help to unload freight aircraft. I remember working outside of my usual shifts to help unload flowers that had come in from the Channel Islands aboard an ABC flight.

"It was a great place to work. I used to get up in the morning and think 'hooray, I've got to go to work'."

Dave Fairweather, who worked with the duty crew during the same period, shared his colleague's view of working at EMA.

He said: "It was a really friendly place to work, everyone got on well together.

Below:
Douglas Bader opens the new runway and terminal extension – 4th May 1970.

Opposite page:
Alan Webb, Chief Fire Officer, watches on as **Eric Dyer** (centre) accepts the delivery of a new fire engine.

Right:
Labour Prime Minister Mr James Callaghan talks to British Midland Airways stewardesses after arriving at East Midlands Airport – 1967.

"We had to do everything. It was a mixed job, but that is what kept it interesting.

"One Christmas Eve I was working the 2 'til 10 shift and getting ready to go home for the holiday.

"The airport closed at 10pm but just before this we got a call to say that two TriStars were coming our way because fog was stopping them from getting into airports in the south.

"We had to provide the hospitality for the passengers until they could get away at 5.30am on Christmas Day.

"As the 1970s progressed the airport got increasingly busy, especially in the summer and at weekends. Often we'd be working to half hour turnarounds.

"Along with the growth in freight traffic this showed that the airport was becoming a big success."

There were other signs of success at the close of a decade that had seen EMA build on its modest beginnings and cement its future.

And by the end of the 1970s few people doubted that EMA was going to play a key part in the region's economy for decades to come.

This was reflected in some of the technical advances seen at the airport.

David Gretton records that the Board of Trade gave their go-ahead for EMA's first runway extension on March 23rd 1970. The runway was to be extended to 7,480 feet and the taxiways widened to 75 feet.

He said: "The extension of the runway was carried out by A Monk and Company at a cost of £500,000. It caused the closure of the B5401 Swan Rivers road between Castle Donington and Diseworth.

"One of the first aircraft to use the new facilities was an Andover of the Queen's Flight, which brought in Princess Alexandra for an official engagement in Burton-on-Trent.

"A few days later, just in time for the Easter rush, the new facilities in the passenger concourse came into use. These included the 150-seat One-Eleven Restaurant, a self-service cafeteria, a new bar, and a conference room."

Above:
Captain Mike Hibberd showing youngsters around the Partenavia P68 Ryburn Air Taxi – 1978.

Left:
Swans launch a holiday programme from East Midlands Airport – 1976.

1970

**Runway extension
to 7,480 feet**

March 1970

**Lockheed L1011 TriStar arrives
at East Midlands Airport**

July 1971

Cargo Terminal 2 opens

1973

**6th edition of airport
official handbook
published**

1974

1970

1970

Edward Heath elected as
British Prime Minister

First Jumbo Jets enter service

1973

Britain, Ireland and Denmark join EEC

1974

Harold Wilson elected as
British Prime Minister

Gerald Ford elected as
US President

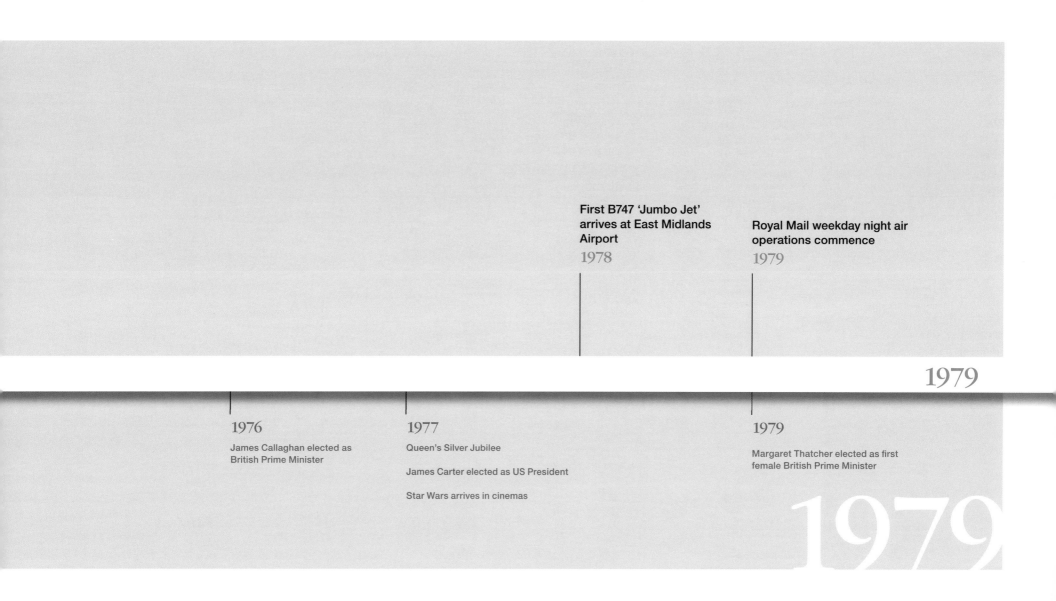

First B747 'Jumbo Jet' arrives at East Midlands Airport
1978

Royal Mail weekday night air operations commence
1979

1979

1976

James Callaghan elected as British Prime Minister

1977

Queen's Silver Jubilee

James Carter elected as US President

Star Wars arrives in cinemas

1979

Margaret Thatcher elected as first female British Prime Minister

1979

Right:
Off on holiday from East Midlands Airport.

Previous pages:
Aerial view of EMA from the mid-1970s.

Along with the improvements to the terminal runway and taxiways, the airport's navigational aids were also substantially uprated in the early 1970s.

The sixth edition of East Midlands Airport's Official Handbook, published in 1974, paints a clear picture of the airport's development since its opening.

It states: "The work (to extend the runway) involved the filling-in of the natural valley with approximately 90,000 cubic yards of pulverised fuel ash and the laying of almost 70,000 square yards of reinforced concrete to the same design as that used on the original scheme.

"The recently improved terminal building, which runs parallel to the apron and allows easy access to and from the airside and landside approaches, has, among other things, a 150-seat restaurant on the first floor, two well-stocked bars, a lounge, a cafeteria capable of seating 80 people, a spacious conference room which is becoming more and more popular with industrialists, and a viewing balcony overlooking the apron.

"In general, the building, which is of a CLASP construction, is divided into four sections – the concourse block, the customs block, the services and control block, and the transit sheds."

It concludes with a firm endorsement of EMA's performance.

"The East Midlands Airport certainly seems to be heading in the right direction.

"However, although it is too early to assess the true impact of an airport on the area, it is fair to say that its record to date of continuing expansion has proved an ability to cater for the needs of its catchment area and it stands as a fine example of first class co-operation and partnership by local authorities."

Praise indeed!

John Baddiley explained additional technical improvements at EMA. He said: "At the time of the installation of the state-of-the-art Plessey STAN 37-38 Instrument Landing System (ILS) in 1970, the Charlie-Alpha Non-Directional Beacon was uprooted from its position near Kegworth railway station and moved to a site next to the Outer

Marker at East Leake. This change meant that aircraft could use new holding and let-down procedures.

"The ILS transmitted invisible radio guidance beams along the centreline of the runway and up at three degrees from the touchdown point, out to as far as 25 miles from the Airport.

"This was a 'precision approach' system and enabled pilots, or more likely the aircraft autopilot, to fly very accurate and stable approaches time-after-time whatever the weather conditions.

"The Outer Marker was installed in a field just off West Leake Road in East Leake and gave the pilot a dah-dah-dah-dah sound in his headphones and a blue flashing light on his instrument panel.

"All was then silent until the aircraft passed over a field near Molehill Farm at Kegworth, a range of 1,020 metres from the start of the runway, when the pilot got a dit-dah-dit-dah-dit-dah and an amber flashing light on the instrument panel. This signalled the passing of the Middle Marker.

Left:
Alderman Mrs Anne Yates (right) with the first half millionth passenger in a year – December 1972.

Below:
One Eleven Restaurant – 1972.

Above:
Sir Michael Bishop began his airline career at Manchester Airport in 1963 by setting up an aircraft handling business for a locally based airline. When the airline was taken over in 1964 by British Midland Airways, he joined the new company and has remained there ever since.

Right:
Derbyshire celebrity Ted Moult hands cuddly toys to children embarking on the first Horizon Holidays flight – April 1971.

"By this time the aircraft was over the start of the high-intensity Category 2 approach lighting system. If the lights could be seen the autopilot was disconnected and the last 1,000 metres could be flown visually and the landing completed manually.

"If it was bad weather and the pilot couldn't see the lights, a missed approach procedure was invoked and the aircraft could either make another approach or divert to a different airport.

"This procedural flying is still usable today and rookie airline pilots have to prove they can follow self-flown let-down procedures, without radar guidance from Air Traffic Control, in order to pass their Instrument Ratings examinations."

From the outset, British Midland Airways, now BMI, has had a presence at EMA.

Sir Michael Bishop, Chairman of BMI, said: "We have enjoyed a very constructive relationship with EMA for the past 40 years and I would like to think that we will still be operating out of the airport in 40 years' time."

The relationship between BMI and EMA continues to be important to the East Midlands Region today and BMI, under the leadership of Nigel Turner, is building a still greater presence at the airport.

British Midland moved their operations from Burnaston Airfield near Derby once EMA was up and running.

Eileen Derrick started work for British Midland two weeks before the move and then worked for the airline at East Midlands Airport for more than 16 years.

She said: "To be fair it was a bit like Fred Karno's Circus to start with but in a short space of time it became a very professional operation.

"The 1970s saw the real growth of air travel and at East Midlands we worked very long hours to meet the demand.

"It was a great place to work."

Monica Snowden was also in the thick of the growth seen in holiday flights.

Above:
The British Rugby Team fly out on tour from East Midlands Airport.

Above:
View of the terminal front.

Right:
John Day, Assistant Airport Director (left) receives a commemorative photograph of the first Jumbo to land at EMA.

She worked initially for Clarkson Holidays before having three years with Horizon Holidays at the end of the decade.

"It was a very friendly place to work. We were all like one big happy family," she said.

"Clarkson were very much pioneers in the holiday market and started by flying people abroad on 38-seater DC3 Dakotas. It was not long before the demand grew and the planes got bigger.

"Before the war most people never went abroad; that was just for the rich and famous.

"But by the 1970s people were beginning to think of taking their summer holiday in Spain.

"Once the numbers started to grow it was very hard work. Most people had never experienced flying before and many of them were nervous about it.

"I don't like flying myself but always did my best to reassure them.

"There was a patch of four-leaf clover just outside the terminal building and I picked a piece myself.

"Perhaps I should have opened a little stall and sold them for luck. It would have been a good business."

Another aircraft that made use of EMA's newly-extended runway in 1971 was the Lockheed L1011 TriStar.

The development of the RB211 engines for the aircraft at Rolls Royce in Derby guaranteed massive local interest.

However, it is still hard to imagine the level of excitement that the arrival of the first TriStar at EMA brought to the region.

The aircraft flew into the airport on Thursday June 3rd 1971 and left the following Monday.

During that brief stay thousands of people queued for hours to get a close up look at the TriStar, whose development had impacted directly on the East Midlands' economic health.

Nick Walker, a designer at Rolls Royce in Derby, remembers the emotions of the day he got a close-up look at the TriStar.

Left:
Thousands give their verdict on the Lockheed TriStar: 'She's a great airplane!' – June 1971.

Right:
The Duty Crew of 1976 (from left to right):
Steve Brylinski, John Smith, Alan Heaps,
Barry West, Ron Priest, Jake Mrugaez,
George Watts, Ian Hole, an unknown
and Roy Tacey.

"There were times when the development of the TriStar's RB211 engines seemed to threaten the very existence of Rolls Royce.

"Everyone who worked in the company's aircraft division invested so much skill, hard work and emotion into the project that there was no way we were going to miss out on the chance to see the plane up close.

"Like thousands of others I queued for hours for my chance to walk through the cabin. Even though we were only on board the aircraft for minutes it was worth the wait. I was so proud," he said.

Duty crew member Owen Ward remembers well the day the TriStar came to EMA: "I was the one with the bats out on the apron helping the pilot to park up.

"He'd flown over the Rolls Royce factory in Derby to give the workers a good look at the aircraft before making his approach to the airport.

"Thousands of people from the local area came out to the airport to get a good look at the aircraft."

The Rolls Royce RB211 engines would prove to be excellent workhorses but the TriStar was introduced at a time of rampant inflation and in direct competition with another trijet, the Douglas DC-10. It proved to be Lockheed's last foray into the passenger jet market place.

It was also in 1971 that EMA was given its own section of controlled airspace.

John Baddiley explains: "A Control Zone, going from the ground upwards, and a Control Area, going upwards from defined heights or altitudes above EMA, ensure that Air Traffic Control has absolute power over all aircraft in the locality. It became a legal requirement for all pilots to be in radio contact with ATC whilst flying in controlled airspace. Safety was improved as, in theory, all air traffic was known about.

"However, to use the new airspace fully and ensure safe separation of aircraft, and to detect the presence of aircraft not in radio contact, a more-effective and longer-range radar system

was needed to augment the airport's original 424, which had been developed in the 1950s from marine radar used on ships."

A decision was taken to purchase an AR1 Surveillance Radar system from Plessey, who were based in the Isle of Wight.

This system was used extensively both in civil aviation throughout the world and at all RAF bases at the time.

John Baddiley again: "The AR1 was installed near where the east cargo apron is to be found today.

"Detected radar signals were fed via underground cables to new displays in the airport's control tower. The old radar 'cupboard' display room was extended to accommodate the 424 displays already in use and two new AR1 displays. The AR1 offered clutter cancellation, so all that ATC controllers saw on their screens was moving aircraft, not a myriad of reflections from hills and weather formations. This made radar control of aircraft much easier, with a bright yellow blip showing their positions."

Above:
Cars everywhere as people seek the best vantage point to see the TriStar – Whit Sunday, 1971.

Right:

Passengers disembark from an
Air France Concorde – 1979.

Far left:
Inside the control tower.

Left and below:
Runway and apron extensions under construction.

Right:
A young Prince Charles visits
the airport – February 1971.

Another new radar system was to be introduced before the turn of the 1980s, but more of that later.

New technology was also arriving in the terminal building.

We have all stood transfixed looking at departure and arrival boards in our time. At the beginning of the 1970s, EMA introduced its first flapper board, a term that becomes clear when you think back to the days before screen displays.

"When the airport opened, a large flapper board had been installed on the east wall of the terminal building (between where the Aviation Hobby Shop and Boots stand today)," said John Baddiley.

"The board was a very complicated electro-mechanical device that had an arrivals column and a departures column, both of which displayed times alongside each entry.

"The arrivals and departures columns each had about a dozen slots. In each slot was an array of thin metal plates with the names of airports etched on them. It was the job of the information desk staff to use a box of multi-position thumbwheels to flap the plates by remote control until the correct airport was displayed in the correct window with the correct time next to it."

Mr Baddiley revealed that the board was prone to seizure as it attracted dust into its mechanism and had a very delicate electrical system.

If you stood and watched the board being updated you could be taken on an amazing whistle-stop tour of the world. Dozens of airports would click briefly into view as the board flapped between Amsterdam and Zurich, pass-ing all alphabetical points in-between.

In his annual report of 1979/80, Airport Director Eric Dyer was able to reveal a 13.9 percent increase in cargo passing through the airport.

He also said: "A new achievement at the airport during the year was the inclusion of 870,807 kgs of PO Mail carried by the recently implemented Post Office service during the night hours."

NEMA Cargo Manager Bill

Blanchard has revealed that this was far from a planned development but rather a case of EMA responding to an urgent requirement.

"Prior to this time the mail was moved north by night-train to Scotland. However a tunnel collapse left the Royal Mail urgently looking for an alternative," he said.

"They quickly spotted EMA's great location in relation to motorway routes and commenced night flights of mail from the airport.

"Like much of EMA's initial cargo operations, this came about purely as a response to a need. Cargo Terminal 2 was in operation and ELAN, who later integrated with DHL (who were then very much just document carriers), were active at the airport.

"In the 1970s Rolls Royce were using EMA to ship their RB211 engines out to Lockheed in America, but it was not until towards the end of the decade that the true cargo potential of EMA was showing itself. We now move as much cargo in a month as we did in a year back in the early 1980s."

Above:
The upstairs bar and lounge – 1977.

Left:
Filming BBC TV programme 'Play Away' starring Brian Cant as the pilot.

Right:
BMA check-in desks late 1970s.

The 1970s was a period of sustained growth for East Midlands Airport. It was the decade that added the cement to the foundations put down in 1965.

That the current airport operation still stands largely upon those foundations is testament to the hard work of many people throughout those years.

Figures published in 1979 tell the story.

Annual passenger numbers began the decade at 288,150, rising to 565,441 by 1975 and ending the 1970s at 593,587.

Thomson Holidays referred to EMA as "one of our top performers" and noted that "in the past year or so there was a marked increase in the number of people from Leicester and district specifying East Midlands as a departure point".

1,586 tonnes of air cargo were handled in 1970, rising to 8,321 tonnes by 1975. After a dip from this mid-decade high point, there was a total of 6,283 tonnes handled in 1979.

Based on this growth, Eric Dyer already had his sights firmly fixed on another runway extension.

Councillor Walter Marshall laid out the case when he said: "The further extension of the runway is vital for the future economic growth of the area, particularly at a time when there is talk of world recession and our businessmen are having to travel further afield and more often in search of orders.

"And, having won the orders, they must then have confidence that the transport system by air can deliver the goods on time."

Leicestershire County Council had turned down the airport's planning application for a runway extension to nearly 9,500 feet, forcing the issue to a public inquiry in October 1981.

Although it must have been a frustrating time for Eric Dyer, his characteristic reserve came through as he concluded his annual report and closed the 1970s with these words: "We look forward with intense interest to the forthcoming public inquiry into the runway extension and, should our forecasts prove once again to be correct, to producing yet again another record year during 1980/81, which in turn would serve to benefit the region as a whole."

Following pages:
Air France Concorde heads out for departure – 1979.

Right:
Margaret Thatcher signs the visitor book
during a visit to East Midlands Airport
in 1979, the year she became the first
female Prime Minister.

Left:
Check-in Hall showing the new
'state-of-the-art' flapper display boards
in the top left corner of the picture.

Right:
Crossroads' Meg Richardson,
played by Noele Gordon at
East Midlands Airport – July 1979.

Far right:
Les Dawson filming at the airport – 1974.

Left:
Valerie Carter, Chief Receptionist, models the new uniform – 1978.

Far left:
The Red Arrows with their Folland Gnat aircraft were frequent visitors to East Midlands Airport – 1978.

Chapter Three | 1980-1989

ON A COLD Friday in December 1986, HRH Princess Anne, now the Princess Royal, opened a £3.8 million terminal extension at East Midlands Airport. It was 21 years since her father had officially opened the original terminal building.

Demand had brought about the development. Just a year earlier, the airport had announced that – for the first time – more than a million passengers had passed through its doors during a financial year.

The growth in the demand for foreign holidays, a major cultural shift that has been gathering pace since the early 1970s, was driving the upward trend in passenger numbers.

Change was in the air at EMA, both in the way the airport was run and in what it aspired to be.

Councillor Joe Murphy, Chairman of the EMA Joint Committee, said at the time that the financial year 1984/85 had been the most successful in the airport's 19-year history.

Writing in the airport's annual report, Councillor Murphy stated: "Passenger traffic through the airport rose by 10 percent from 988,960 to 1,083,987 while air cargo increased by 58 percent from 8,769 tonnes to 13,853 tonnes."

Airport Director Eric Dyer went further. "The twentieth year of the operation of the airport has been possibly the most significant in its history, with a total in excess of one million passengers being catered for on its public transport flights, and a growth in both mail and freight which led to its recent classification as '... the provincial airport with the greatest growth during the year...'."

Mr Dyer continued: "This activity has led to the largest profit for its shareholding local authorities since the original investment, and also prompted the airport's Joint Committee to authorise the expenditure of more than £3 million to extend and modernise its passenger facilities – an enormous task which is well under way.

"These extensions will cater for up to 1.5 million passengers a year and will offer the most up to date amenities prior to and subsequent to their flight."

The numbers were starting to grow and, whilst this demonstrated the success of the East Midlands' own regional airport, it also began to raise questions about the financial cost of future development driven by growing demand.

EMA's growth was gathering pace but, if the airport was to achieve its full potential, it would require levels of ongoing investment that would test the local authorities who owned the airport.

Colin Sorrell, today the Development Support Manager at NEMA, was in a good position to watch these commercial pressures build, given that he worked for Leicestershire County Council between 1982 and 1997.

He said: "There appeared to be both an inability and a reluctance to invest in the airport to the degree that was required.

"The Joint Committee ran an airport of regional significance and there was a lot of debate about the significance of what the airport brought to the region."

Above:
Princess Anne arrives at EMA to open the terminal extension – December 1986.

Opposite page:
Three Laker DC10 wide bodied jets arrive within the space of one hour. However, to operate commercially from EMA, these aircraft would need the proposed longer runway – June 1980.

Right:
The 112-bedroomed Donington Thistle Hotel has been on the Airport since it arrived in kit form in 1986. It opened for business in 1987.

"Decisions through committees took a lot of time in the context of a commercial enterprise that was moving forward at a growing rate."

Mr Sorrell, who worked in Leicestershire County Council's Estate Services department, was also involved in another high-profile development on the airport site.

"The Thistle Hotel that opened in January 1987 had been an aspiration for the airport for some time. But the negotiations that eventually led to the hotel being built were very long and complex, with private investment being made at a publicly owned airport," said Mr Sorrell.

The 4-star Donington Thistle Hotel cost £4 million to develop and offered 112 bedrooms, conference facilities, meeting rooms, a restaurant and a bar. There was also a swimming pool and other leisure facilities.

The words of Councillor John Heppell, then Chairman of the Joint Committee, echo Colin Sorrell's view.

He recorded at the time: "An airport hotel has been a distant dream for many years but now the reality will greatly assist the airport in its future development."

It also fell to Councillor Heppell to acknowledge another landmark in the history of EMA in the Annual Report of 1985/86.

Eric Dyer retired as Airport Director, although the report itself names him as General Manager following the change of company status, of which more later.

Councillor Heppell said: "Mr Dyer has been with the airport since it began and a special tribute must be paid to him for his part in its successful growth over the years."

Kind as these words were, today they seem insufficient to convey the part played by Eric Dyer in the development of EMA.

Eric Dyer had a vision of how to take something quite insignificant in aviation terms and turn it into a remarkable success.

His own personality set the tone for EMA becoming known as the friendly airport where customer service is right at the forefront of every initiative.

Shortly before his departure in 1986 Mr Dyer wrote: "This final report from me must include my heartfelt gratitude to my employing authority for giving to me, twenty-two years ago, the honour and privilege of being the first Airport Director and enabling me to be 'in' at the beginning of such a marvellous and successful project.

"Its success is attributable to the dedication of the staff, the confidence of the many users and tenant companies and, of course, to the never-failing support of the various constituent authorities. Naturally I hope that I have succeeded in carrying out the task originally assigned to me, and am confident that its success will continue."

It was a changing of the guard, and perhaps a shift of the mood.

Mr Dyer had been the perfect man for dealing with tightly-regulated local authority committees. Speculation as to how he would have fared in today's highly competitive commercial aviation market is just that, pure speculation.

Above:
Eric Dyer, Airport Director – 1964-1986.

1980

**New Jasmin system
introduced at EMA to
log flight movements**

1983

**ELAN operations commence
(now DHL)**

**EMA passed 1m passenger
mark (1.082 million)**

1984

1980

1981

Ronald Reagan elected as US President

First flight of US Space Shuttle, Columbia

IBM launches first PC;
utilising Microsoft Software

1983

Miners strike broken by
Thatcher government

1984

US Space Shuttle
Challenger is launched

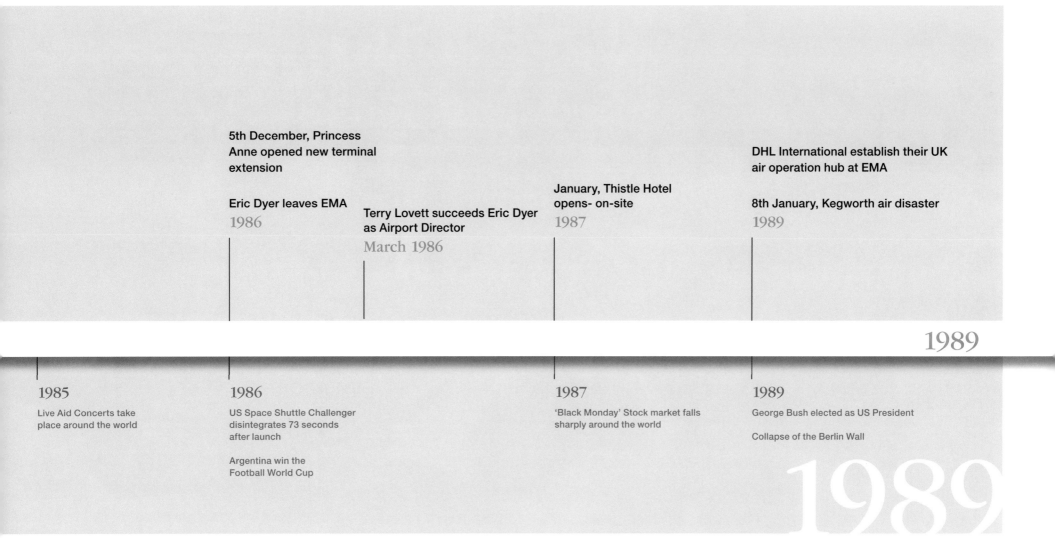

**5th December, Princess
Anne opened new terminal
extension**

**DHL International establish their UK
air operation hub at EMA**

Eric Dyer leaves EMA
1986

**Terry Lovett succeeds Eric Dyer
as Airport Director**
March 1986

**January, Thistle Hotel
opens- on-site**
1987

8th January, Kegworth air disaster
1989

1989

1985

Live Aid Concerts take
place around the world

1986

US Space Shuttle Challenger
disintegrates 73 seconds
after launch

Argentina win the
Football World Cup

1987

'Black Monday' Stock market falls
sharply around the world

1989

George Bush elected as US President

Collapse of the Berlin Wall

1989

Right:
Postmen at work in the middle of the
night at East Midlands Airport.

Previous pages:
In the centre of a vast crowd outside the
arrivals hall, Nottingham Forest captain John
McGovern is seen clutching the European
Cup. Forest had just beaten Malmo (Sweden)
1-0 in the final played in Munich – 1979.

Another change of lasting importance was also on the horizon.

Councillor Heppell revealed his irritation with enforced change in the airport's 1985/86 annual report.

He said: "My last, and possibly most important item of the report, is the privatisation of the airport into a Public Airport Company (PAC). The airport committee has consistently opposed Government proposals for privatisation seeing no reason for the changes except political dogma.

"By next year we will be forced to become a PAC and we have for some time been looking at the consequences of this.

"One consequence is that, in the future, money that was returned to the ratepayers of Nottinghamshire, Derbyshire, Leicestershire and Nottingham City Council will be taken instead by central government through corporation tax, VAT etc.

"I find it disgraceful that local government, after years of bearing the financial risk of the airport, should now have the benefits of their enterprise reduced by central government which has borne no risk in the past and will not in the future. The legislation is only a means to allow the Treasury to dip their fingers into the local government till."

These were strong words giving one side of the argument. Others felt that privatisation would attract external funding that could help East Midlands Airport to achieve its ambitious goals.

The change came about on April 1st 1987 and a restructuring of the airport management team was led by Terry Lovett, who had succeeded Eric Dyer as East Midlands Airport General Manager.

After a disappointing closing year to Mr Dyer's tenure, Mr Lovett was able to reveal that record levels of traffic had been achieved in every sector of the airport's operations since he grasped the reins.

He said: "Total passenger traffic has increased by 22 percent and, specifically in the Inclusive Tour Sector, by 35 percent over 1985/86.

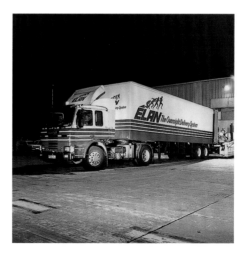

Above:
ELAN (European Land Air Network) Herald Freighter.

Left:
ELAN – early subsidiary of DHL operation at East Midlands Airport.

Above:
Short stay car park – May 1984.

Right:
Apron and taxiway work in progress.

"Air freight and mail together have increased by 28 percent making East Midlands Airport the fourth largest cargo airport in the United Kingdom, with a combined throughput of 27,779 metric tonnes."

Passenger numbers had topped 1.145 million people with a new monthly high of 153,084 passengers achieved in August 1986.

Change had been underway elsewhere at East Midlands Airport since the beginning of the decade. Revolutions were taking place in the electronics world and East Midlands Airport endeavoured to bring some of its systems up to the levels in use at Britain's leading airports.

Complex state-of-the-art radar systems were introduced and new electronic markers installed to guide aircraft on their approach to the airport.

John Baddiley takes up the story of the introduction of technology we all take completely for granted these days but which was truly revolutionary just over 20 years ago.

"A large step forward in flight data electronic equipment took place in 1983," he said.

"Since East Midlands Airport first opened in 1965, all arrival and departure details had been logged on a paper form, in duplicate, by the Tower Air Traffic Assistant.

"This paper log was transferred to the airport's finance section so that aircraft operators could be invoiced for using the airport facilities.

"The new 'Jasmin' system, made by Jasmin electronics in Leicester, was a centralised data processor that electronically logged flight movements.

"It also provided real-time arrivals and departure information for the new information screens in the terminal building."

Your home PC probably has a lot more power – and definitely more speed – but it was a tentative step into the computer age.

Let us look at the story behind the introduction of new meteorological equipment on the airfield.

Left:
De-icing being carried out at
East Midlands Airport – 1983.

Right:
The opening of the new Fire Station.
Pictured from left to right: Graham Hoffman,
John Gilbert, Geoff Webster, Phil Chapman and
Colin Tweed – 1984.

John Baddiley again: "Traditionally, when it was misty or foggy and we needed to measure the visibility along the runway, three firemen were sent to man the three Runway Observation Points (ROPs).

"An ROP looked like a two-storey yellow and white chequered wooden shed. They were situated next to the runway, each covering a third of its length.

"A fireman had to look through a slot and count the number of runway edge lights that were visible along his third of the runway. These lights were 60 metres apart so it was easy to calculate the runway's visible range."

An electronic system that measures the visibility along the runway edge was purchased in 1982. The firemen stood down and the damp, draughty ROP sheds were removed.

Like the ROPs the Instrumental Runway Visual Range (IRVR) System had three measuring points, or heads, with each measuring how much a beam of red light was being attenuated (reduced), by the amount of water droplets in the air.

The more the reduction the thicker the fog. On a clear day the attenuation figure would be nil.

Of course, knowing there is fog is one thing. Landing an aircraft in it is another matter altogether.

And, after landing, there is the problem of guiding an aircraft off the runway and back along taxiways, often working with a pilot who does not know the airport.

EMA undertook a major investment project in 1988/89 to upgrade its airfield lighting. All the work to install the lighting took place through the night so as not to disrupt EMA's daily schedule.

John Baddiley takes up the story: "New high-intensity runway centreline lights spaced 15 metres apart were installed, as were new approach lights on both ends of the runway.

"There was also a new guidance system that allowed air traffic controllers to switch blocks of green taxiway centreline lights on and off.

Above:
Orion 'Aircraft Pull' helping raise hundreds of pounds for the BBC's Children in Need appeal.

Left:
Hostess for a day: 12-year-old Deborah Cracknell from Loughborough – September 1987.

"This enabled the selection of taxiway routes from the runway to the apron, and vice-versa, during bad weather.

"All a pilot now had to do was 'follow the greens' of the taxiway route that was illuminated for him and be guided around the airport. Red illuminated stop bars could also be switched on to stop aircraft straying onto the runway or into another sector of the taxiway already occupied by another aircraft."

Former British Midland pilot David Moores says his affection for EMA remains undiminished as he enjoys his retirement.

Mr Moores, who lives in nearby Diseworth, believes he flew the third commercial flight into EMA on the airport's first day of operation back in 1965 after transferring from Burnaston Airport.

He said: "For a pilot, East Midlands was always a pretty easy airport to fly in and out of. There are no major obstacles, although occasionally you would find yourself held up over Lincolnshire by a light aircraft approach or the postal service flights.

"Air traffic control were also pretty easy to deal with. If you could see the airfield they were comfortable with you making a visual approach.

"EMA became less user-friendly over the years I was there; it was inevitable really as the airport got busier. In the 1960s, you would know most people at the airport and there was far less traffic to deal with. It was a relatively quiet municipal airport."

Living in Diseworth, Mr Moores is well aware of the impact the growth of the airport has had on villages close to the Castle Donington site.

"In Diseworth we are parallel to the line of the runway so the aircraft movements do not have quite the impact they do on the people in Castle Donington and Kegworth. These days I do have some sympathy with people living in those villages because of the impact of night flights.

"If you ask whether I thought about the people in Kegworth as I made an approach to East Midlands when I was flying, I'd say the answer is no.

Left:
It was "Full-House" for this Dan-Air Boeing 727 when it left on the first flight of the Exchange holiday programme to Cyprus.

Right:
The B737-300 which came into
service at East Midlands Airport
with Orion Airways in 1985.

Previous pages:
Aerial photo – 1987.

"But then again I wasn't doing it between the hours of 11pm and 7am."

There has been local opposition to EMA since before it opened for commercial operations in 1965. The strength of that opposition has ebbed and flowed in relation to the profile of issues affecting the development of the airport site.

Airport Fire Chief Alan Webb, who worked at the airport from 1965 until the early 1990s, lived in Kegworth for a time but moved out of the village.

Mr Webb said: "Once people learnt that you worked at the airport it was like they thought you could deal with all their complaints."

Former EMA Managing Director John Spooner, now Managing Director at Manchester Airport, lived in Kegworth during the 1990s and had a different view.

"I felt that I couldn't really look people in the eye when talking about airport noise unless I lived close to the airport," he said. Mr Spooner now lives in a village close to the edge of the airfield at Manchester Airport.

Opposition to EMA's operations is sure to continue for as long as aircraft movements continue.

However, 40 years on, the airport has demonstrated that it is here to stay. It is how the relationship between local residents and the airport is managed that presents challenges for the future.

Back in 1987, Terry Lovett announced that £125,000 was to be spent on noise monitoring equipment.

He said: "The noise monitoring points were agreed with local representatives and Parish Councils. The equipment sited there was designed to give read-outs of aircraft noise levels under the flight path and pass the data directly to a computer within our Air Traffic Control Unit.

"These monitoring systems make it possible to identify any aircraft that breaks the limitations."

EMA first introduced spectator facilities in 1979 and these grew in both interest and popularity during the early 1980s. However, the growth of the airport resulted in the closure of this first spectator area in November 1983.

Above:
A big family reunion for three children and their parents, split apart by the troubles in Vietnam – July 1987.

Left:
Football legend Brian Clough, former Deby County and Nottingham Forest Manager, visits East Midlands Airport.

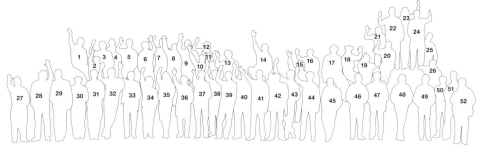

Left:

Staff gather to celebrate EMA's 20th Anniversary (back row, left to right):

1 Jack Rusling, 2 Bill Handley, 3 Bob Shields, 4 Alan Tolson, 5 Iain Inglis, 6 Mick Hodgkin, 7 Bob Paterson,
8 Pete Waters, 9 Frank Rae, 10 John Gunn, 11 Roger Hallam, 12 Albert Paul, 13 David Crowder,
14 Tony Capewell, 15 Colin Thompson, 16 John Brown, 17 Jeff Jackson, 18 George Wright, 19 Ian Jubb,
20 Tony Draycott, 21 Dave Bishop, 22 Dave Shepherd, 23 Eddie Mrugacz, 24 Maurice Corpe,
25 Derek Pillmore, 26 Gordon Walker, 27 Harry Cain, 28 Mick Clampitt, 29 Keith Simpson, 30 Ron Harris,
31 David Pearce, 32 Martin Rollinson, 33 Alan Ackerman, 34 Jean McNish, 35 Jill Shufflebotham,
36 Arthur Snape, 37 Derek Abbey, 38 Eric Clarke, 39 Kevin Marks, 40 Stuart Springett, 41 Dave Eastgate,
42 Dave McInerney, 43 Keith Bennett, 44 Jerry Ryan, 45 Tony Rumsay, 46 Paul Roberts, 47 Alex Temple,
48 John Blacknell, 49 John Baddiley, 50 John Woodise, 51 Mark Chambers, 52 Pete Bell.

Right:
(From left to right) Alan Webb, Eric Dyer, OBE, John Pearson (Derbyshire County Council Civil Engineer), and Duty Officer Roy Tacey receiving their commemorative decanters to mark the airport's 21st Birthday from Terry Lovett (second from right).

Left:
Eric Dyer and Val Carter celebrate
East Midlands Airport's 21st Anniversary.

Right:
EMA Chairman David Wilcox opening Britain's first lounge dedicated for use by holidaymakers – 1986.

Previous pages:
The first B757 to visit EMA flew up from the Farnborough Air Show to show Rolls Royce employees their 'engines on the wing' – September 1982.

Left:
One of the many parties of Travel Agents
to visit the airport – 1988.

Right:
The second man on the moon, Dr Buzz Aldrin, and his wife visit the Field Aircraft Jetstream 31/32 completion facility.

Left:
Diana, Princess of Wales, visits
East Midlands Airport – March 1984.

Right:
Coronation Street's Ken Barlow (actor Bill Roach) talks to ATC cadets at East Midlands Airport.

An Avro Vulcan B.2 bomber was used as the centrepiece of an exciting new project that became known as The East Midlands Aeropark. Costing around £300,000 and sited near the eastern end of the airport, it featured a Visitor Centre, a number of preserved aircraft, and an excellent viewing mound for enthusiasts.

The Aeropark, opened in May 1984, was cared for by the Aeropark Volunteers Association up until 1996, when the growing pace of development looked set to engulf the site.

In the airport's 40th year a new Aeropark, which opened its doors to the public in August 2001 on the western edge of the airfield, welcomed its 50,000th paying visitor.

But, as the 1980s drew to a close, there was another change within the airport business community. One that would assume major significance over the coming years.

In 1984 ELAN, who were a subsidiary of DHL, commenced operations at EMA. Five years later DHL International established their UK air operation hub at the airport and the ELAN name disappeared.

EMA was putting in place pieces of a jigsaw that would enable it to become one of the world's major cargo hubs.

Mail movements continued to rise each year, confirming the wisdom of the decision to develop EMA as a Royal Mail air hub.

When the first year of operation as a Public Airport Company (PAC) came to a close, East Midlands Airport director Terry Lovett was able to report record passenger numbers and a major development involving the mail service.

He said: "The year saw an increase in passenger throughput of 15.2 percent to 1.3 million. During the year, a major ten-year agreement was finalised between the airport company and the Post Office. The airport has agreed to build a £1.2 million apron extension, complete with a new mail sorting facility and landside vehicle yard."

Passenger numbers continued to grow and the foundations were being laid that would support spectacular growth in the air cargo sector.

Above:
A mini being lifted by scissor lift onto a Vickers Merchantman Freighter.

Left:
Mail sorting – November 1982.

Right:
Sunday 8th January 1989: a Boeing 737 carrying 126 pasengers and crew crashed onto the northbound embankment of the M1 motorway with the tragic loss of 47 lives.

Previous pages:
Three British Airways Boeing 747's and a Gulf Air B767 divert to EMA due to bad weather in the London area.

During the 1980s the airport had successfully negotiated a major change in the way it was run.

Few realised at the time that another major change was just a few short years away.

The darkest event in the airport's 40-year history came on the evening of Sunday January 8th 1989.

A British Midland 737-400 that left London Heathrow Airport at 8.00pm en-route to Belfast experienced engine problems and attempted to make an emergency landing at EMA.

But just three quarters of a mile from the runway the aircraft bounced off the embankment on one side of the M1 motorway, skipping over the carriageway and crashing into the embankment on the other side.

Of the 126 people on board, 39 died during the impact and a further eight died later in what became known as the Kegworth Air Disaster.

Former airport director John Spooner said: "This was without a doubt the worst event I was involved in during my time at EMA, and still the memories of it bring great sadness to mind.

"But there is also a degree of pride in the way that the airport staff performed on the night in the face of great difficulties."

Airport Fire Chief Alan Webb, who had been refining emergency procedures since he started work at the airport back in 1965, also takes great pride in the effective response of his men.

"Although you plan for such an event you pray that it never happens. What a terrible night," he said.

Mr Webb received the MBE in the months following the Kegworth Air Disaster.

Above:
Emergency vehicles on the M1 during the Kegworth air disaster.

Left:
Rescue operations at the scene of the air crash.

Chapter Four | 1990-1999

THE 1990s were to prove a decade of massive change at East Midlands Airport; a decade that put in place additional foundations to accommodate the rapid growth we have seen in the new millennium.

As the decade opened, the airport celebrated its 25th anniversary at a time when the airline industry was in the middle of the worst recession in its history.

Nevertheless, East Midlands Airport Managing Director Terry Lovett was able to report a small increase in profit for 1990, a year when passenger numbers actually fell by 12 percent on the previous twelve months.

The early 1990s was an extremely nervous time for the airline business as it wrestled with recession, high interest rates, soaring oil prices driven by unrest in the Middle East, and a reduction in the holiday charter market.

However, Airport Chairman Peter Burgess believed the airport was still making significant progress, particularly in developing its long-term strategy.

Mr Burgess said: "The company has vigorously pursued a number of commercial opportunities as part of the strategy to diversify sources of income.

"A 54-acre high-quality business park on airport land adjacent to the M1 and new M42 extension is the most exciting potential development."

Looking to the future of the airport, Mr Burgess said: "It is capable of tremendous growth over the coming years to meet demand for more passenger and freight services from our catchment area, stretching from north London to Yorkshire."

Talk of these ambitious plans for the coming 15 years brought to the fore the question of just how major projects could be funded. Did the four local authorities that owned the airport – Derbyshire, Leicestershire and Nottinghamshire County Councils along with Nottingham City Council – have the necessary financial resources?

In 1992, when a major terminal extension was proposed, the owning authorities, who had supported previous developments, said they could not fund the project.

John Baddiley, Nottingham East Midlands Airport's Airfield Engineering Supervisor, remembers well the uncertainty over the airport's future and about how major projects were going to be funded.

Mr Baddiley said: "There were rumours and counter-rumours that the council owners of East Midlands Airport were seriously thinking about selling off their shares to the private sector.

"A period of 'make do and mend' descended on the airport whilst the debate continued about what the changes might mean."

There was also Government pressure on local authorities to reduce their levels of public spending at that time.

The situation came to a head in early 1993, with the local authority shareholders taking a bold decision that led to East Midlands Airport becoming the first major regional airport in the UK to enter the private sector.

Right:
To mark the 25th Anniversary, East Midlands Airport staff from the customer services and marketing departments show off the new-look uniforms.

Left:
David Bellamy receives a bottle of Irish Whiskey from Claire Allen (right), on the occasion of the first CityJet flight from EMA to Dublin.

1990

1990

Royal Mail commence a
Sunday night operation

September 1992

Airport is privatised and
bought by The National
Express Group

August 1993

1990

Nelson Mandela released from prison

German reunification

Iraq invades Kuwait – Gulf War begins

Margaret thatcher resigns –
John Major becomes British Prime Minister

1991

Internet made available for
unrestricted commercial use

1993

Bill Clinton elected as
US President

1994

Channel Tunnel opened
between England
and France

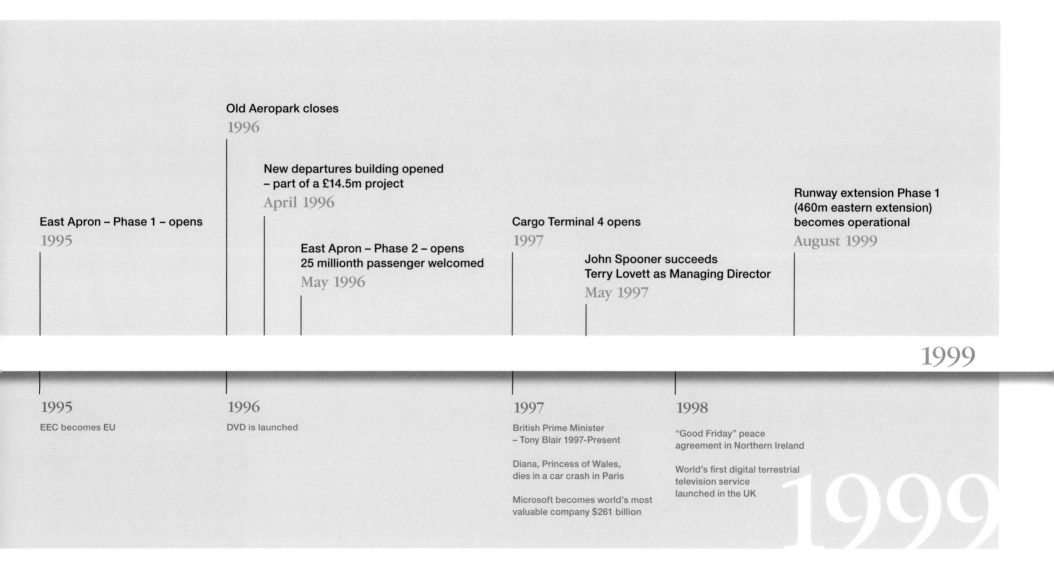

Old Aeropark closes
1996

**New departures building opened
– part of a £14.5m project**
April 1996

East Apron – Phase 1 – opens
1995

**East Apron – Phase 2 – opens
25 millionth passenger welcomed**
May 1996

Cargo Terminal 4 opens
1997

**John Spooner succeeds
Terry Lovett as Managing Director**
May 1997

**Runway extension Phase 1
(460m eastern extension)
becomes operational**
August 1999

1999

1995
EEC becomes EU

1996
DVD is launched

1997
British Prime Minister
– Tony Blair 1997-Present

Diana, Princess of Wales,
dies in a car crash in Paris

Microsoft becomes world's most
valuable company $261 billion

1998
"Good Friday" peace
agreement in Northern Ireland

World's first digital terrestrial
television service
launched in the UK

1999

On Friday 6th August 1993, the National Express Group purchased EMA for £24.3 million, ushering in an eight-year period of investment that dramatically changed the face of the airport.

Ray McEnhill, Chief Executive of National Express, was named the new non-executive Chairman of East Midlands Airport, with Terry Lovett continuing as Managing Director and leading a team of Executive Directors that included Alan Edwards, Patrick Sides, and the newly-appointed executive directors Brian Ratcliffe and future East Midlands Airport Managing Director John Spooner.

Deputy Managing Director Patrick Sides, seen by some people as a future Managing Director of EMA, died suddenly in early 1995 at the age of 43, an event of great sadness for John Spooner.

"Patrick was a great leader who was terrific at bringing people on. I believe he was the natural successor to Terry Lovett.

"His death was one of the saddest moments I experienced whilst working at EMA," said Mr Spooner.

In August 1993, the question in everyone's mind was just what kind of relationship would exist between the new owners and the airport.

Mr McEnhill moved quickly to allay any fears.

He said: "I believe in many ways East Midlands Airport is the ideal airport. Its location is near perfect. Motorway road access is superb.

"There is a large local catchment area. The site and operation is as environmentally friendly as any airport could be.

"The airport is also well managed. Terry Lovett and his team have extensive experience of running airports in general and East Midlands in particular. I believe in letting managers manage. We will do just that, to ensure the continued growth and profitability of the airport."

Terry Lovett accepted that the period leading up to the sale had been a difficult one for everyone employed at the airport.

Right:
A UK regional airport first. Air Foyle AN-124 at EMA on 10th September 1991. Its record-breaking 57.5 ton load is about to be off-loaded from the front of the aircraft.

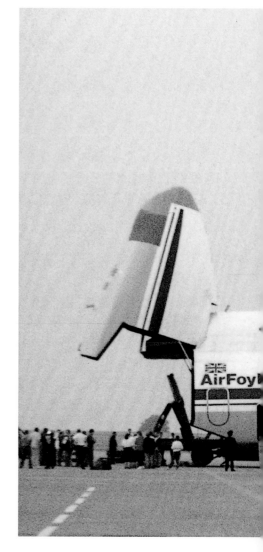

Right:
East Midlands Aiport sponsored
The World Airship Championships - 1990.

Mr Lovett said: "This has been a difficult period for our staff. Uncertainty over the ownership of the company has led to real concern over jobs, pensions and the future role of the airport.

"Morale strengthened as a result of more management/employee joint working and improved communications. We must now maintain the momentum and cohesion.

"National Express Group have given us the opportunity to manage the business within their overall control. This will give us more managerial flexibility. All the signs are that business is picking up, the staff are enthusiastic and the prospects are good."

John Spooner, now Managing Director at Manchester Airport, looks back at the period with a great deal of pride.

"East Midlands is a family airport where the overriding characteristic amongst the staff is a can do attitude. National Express were very supportive and everyone working at the airport was determined not to let them down.

"I look back with great satisfaction.

When I left EMA there was pretty much everything in place that the airport will require for its development over the next 20 years.

"It was all made possible by a team of fantastic, brilliant people."

For Sue Underwood, General Manager Sales & Marketing at EMA during this period, the experience of working in the private sector was a liberating one.

"I never found it easy to go to meetings when the airport was in local authority hands. A few of the councillors found it difficult to accept a woman in any sort of decision-making position. I remember sitting at the back while everyone else sat around a large boardroom table.

"But all that changed when National Express took control. People were allowed to bring their ideas to the fore and talent, that had perhaps been untapped before, now played an important part in driving the company forward in what was becoming an ever-more competitive aviation market place."

Left:
Terminal building showing the new branding launched in Dec 1994.

Below:
British Midland aircraft – September 1995.

Barry Thompson, NEMA's Finance Director and Deputy Managing Director, has a clear view of the change that private ownership brought about at the airport.

Mr Thompson said: "National Express gave people empowerment.

"They made their investment in the first place because they thought they would see a return. They had a belief in the airport's ability to expand and a belief that the airport staff could deliver that expansion."

National Express invested £77 million into the airport infrastructure during the eight years of their ownership, with the most significant developments being the completion of a £20 million runway extension and £3.5 million invested in a new control tower that has become a real regional landmark.

Eric Dyer had actually secured planning permission to extend the runway back in the early 1980s, but the work was never started and the planning permission had lapsed by the time National Express took control.

The planning process was revisited in the mid-1990s with permission eventually granted to allow the airport to lengthen and widen the runway in both the easterly and westerly directions, and with provision for a full-length taxiway.

John Baddiley said: "The older, central section of the runway was also to be resurfaced, as the original concrete was showing signs of decay. Of course, the bottom line was that the airport had to remain operational throughout the duration of the work. This was not an easy task as the extensions had to mate with the existing runway and the resurfacing work would require a lot of plant and tar-laying vehicles on the runway at certain times."

The spring of 1999 saw the REXO (Runway Extension and Overlay) project get underway. An extensive planning period had preceded the project given that work at the easterly end of the runway would inevitably take the runway and its approach lighting towards Kegworth village and the busy surrounding road network.

John Baddiley: "A major headache was the decision as to what would happen to the approach lighting at the Kegworth end of the runway.

"The lighting system needed to extend for 900 metres away from the landing threshold of the runway and maintain a pre-determined layout governed by international regulations.

"The lighting would need to be moved 300 metres away from the airport towards Kegworth and actually straddle the A453 dual carriageway and the M1 motorway. This required the design of some sort of structure so that the lights that straddled the M1 cutting could be serviced. Complex gantries and even a bridge design were eventually discarded because of the fear of something falling onto the motorway. In the end, a simple steel lattice tower system was installed, but this in effect marooned a triple array of centreline lights on a mast, slap bang in the central reservation of the country's busiest motorway, making maintenance difficult.

Opposite page:
National Express coaches pose with Britannia Aircraft, as part of an awareness campaign to highlight their substantial investment at EMA.

Right:
The Maintenance Department 1993, pose in
their new uniforms.
Top row (left to right): Stuart Springett,
Trevor Adcock, Tony Rumsay, Roger Hallam,
Stan Vickers, Bob Shields, Iain Inglis,
Eddie Mrugacz, Jerry Ryan, Colin Thompson,
Gordon Walker, Dick Marshall, Jeff Jackson,
John Brown, Ian Jubb, George Wright,
Derek Pillmore and Mick Read.
Bottom row (left to right):
Keith Bennett, Frank Rae, Maurice Corpe,
Simon Allard, Mick Hodgkin, Kevin Marks and
John Gunn.

"The solution was to install six lights instead of the normal three. Then, if any of the three main lights failed, one of the standby lights could be switched on. Maintenance is carried out whenever the Highways Agency closes the outside lanes of the motorway to service their lighting."

The REXO project was completed in three phases.

Phase one was a 430-metre extension of the eastern third of the runway. Arrivals making an approach from the east would then fly over a safety buffer zone before touching down.

Phase two was a 180-metre extension of the western third of the runway.

This left the most difficult phase of the work until last – the resurfacing and widening of the middle section of the runway. At times, the available runway length was not sufficient to accommodate commercial aircraft, so EMA took the decision to close the runway completely for a number of Saturdays during quiet periods of

the season so that the work could be completed.

The extension project was completed as the 1990s drew to a close. Now, at 2,893 metres, the runway is the sixth longest in the UK.

In April 1999, EMA's spectacular new air traffic control tower became operational. It is currently the second highest in the UK, standing an imposing 52.3 metres above the runway level.

Barry Thompson believes its construction had a fundamental effect on the way people viewed East Midlands Airport.

He said: "The development of the new control tower was symbolic of the ambition of the airport."

In fact, right from the point at which the runway extension project had been defined, it had been obvious that the existing tower would be inadequate.

"We realised the planned developments would compromise the view from the existing control tower that had been in operation since 1965. Air traffic controllers would not be able to see enough of the airfield."

Left:
Engineering department vehicle.

Below:
Work being carried out on pavement edge lights.

Right:
The new control tower
takes shape over a period
of ten days in 1999.

Left:
View, from the apron, of the new
control tower under construction.

Above:
British Airways Boeing 747 weather diversion to EMA – February 1992.

Clearly this was not acceptable from a safety point of view." said John Baddiley.

"The new control tower and its associated base building represented another major investment by National Express, with the total cost being £3.5 million," he said.

Mr Baddiley remembers it as an emotional time for those who had worked within the old control tower for so many years.

The staff canteen, affectionately known as 'the Greasy Spoon', was knocked down in preparation for the building project, as was the boiler house that stood adjacent to the old control tower.

Perhaps this was not so keenly missed given that the boiler house chimneys, for many years the highest structures on the airport site, used to deposit coarse black and yellow dust over the control tower equipment.

"The method of construction for the new control tower was called 'slipform'," said Mr Baddiley.

"A mould was constructed on the foundations that took the same shape as the cross-sectional profile of the completed tower stem. Concrete was poured into the mould, which slowly lifted itself up at the same rate that the concrete set. The mould rose as the concrete at the bottom had set hard enough to support the weight of the whole structure. This process continued until the stem was in place.

"The next step was to dismantle the mould so that construction of the Visual Control Room (VCR) could start. A slab of concrete was built at the top of the stem to take the weight of the VCR and provide a solid base for the construction.

"All the steelwork was raised piece-by-piece by a huge crane and actually built in-situ by a gang of steel erectors. The heaviest and most delicate components were the eight special anti-glare and heated glass panels for the windows," he said.

The dramatic new structure certainly captured the imagination of airport visitors, with 1,500 local residents visiting the tower before the official opening took place.

Even today, there is no shortage of requests for a chance to climb the steps to the top and enjoy the panoramic view of the airfield and the surrounding area.

Drama was certainly the order of the day when the new control tower was officially opened. But not at East Midlands Airport: this drama took place over fields close to the Leicestershire village of Long Whatton. It involved former East Midlands Airport Managing Director John Spooner, who is a keen amateur pilot with his own light aircraft at the airport.

Following the opening ceremony Mr Spooner offered the control tower designer a short flight over the local area, which would no doubt provide a better view of his creation.

Not long after take-off, engine problems developed that caused oil to spray onto the windshield accompanied by thick black smoke that obscured Mr Spooner's view.

"I think the engine's on fire," he radioed back to EMA.

Left:
The new Air Traffic Control Tower shortly after completion.

Above:
**UPS DC8 freighter at
East Midlands Airport – 1994.**

However, Mr Spooner managed to skip over a number of hedges in his aircraft before crash-landing in a field near Long Whatton. The airport fire crew were soon on hand at the crash scene.

Mr Spooner recalled: "A fire officer spotted me standing away from the crash site and said 'you got here quick John'.

"'First here actually', was my immediate response".

What happened to the old control tower?

It is still there if you look closely. A number of ideas were considered for its future use, and it eventually became the base for EMA operations staff. It is used as a lookout tower for bird control officers, apron safety staff and aircraft parking allocation operatives.

Perhaps the most spectacular area of growth in the airport's operations during the 1990s was the cargo sector.

Back in 1994, Terry Lovett recorded the importance of this when he said: "One of the most exciting developments in 1994 has been the progress that East Midlands Airport has made towards becoming one of the world's major cargo airports.

"In August 1993, United Parcel Service (UPS) moved to East Midlands to create their new UK hub, operating initially from temporary accommodation.

"In March 1994, their new buildings were opened by David Hunt MP, then Employment Minister. UPS had previously operated from five UK airports but has now consolidated all activities into one air-hub at East Midlands, attracted by our proven ability to handle express parcel traffic and our geographical location in the heart of England.

"Allied to this has been the dramatic growth in DHL's operations through the airport and the commencement of regular nightly scheduled cargo services by Lufthansa.

"As a result of all this, freight and mail throughput at East Midlands rose by 75 percent in 1994. Pure cargo (carried on dedicated freighter aircraft) rose by 92 percent. We entered the list of the world's top 100 cargo airports and were the second-fastest growing cargo airport in the world.

"To meet this growth in demand, £2.5 million was spent on the provision of a new cargo apron to the east of the fire station. Plans were also drawn up for a fourth cargo terminal and a large site was leased to DHL for the extension and development of Cargo Terminal 2."

Since then East Midlands Airport has become the UK's No.1 airport for handling pure cargo.

It was in 1994 that Mr Lovett also revealed plans for a major redevelopment of the airport's check-in hall, along with proposed upgrades to the departure baggage system, an extension of the international arrivals area with an additional baggage reclaim unit, and the redevelopment of car parks and roads that would serve the new terminal.

There was also to be a complete refurbishment and redevelopment of the terminal building. The total cost for all this work was estimated to be £9.8 million.

Left:
John Spooner receiving the CAA Safety
Award from HRH Prince Michael of Kent.

Above:
John Spooner's Robin aircraft close to
Long Whatton.

Right:
Avro Vulcan on display at the old
Aeropark which opened in May 1984.
A new site opened in August 2001.

Left:
Simon Groom, the children's television presenter, is seen by some of his fans after opening a £20,000 children's play area on the old Aeropark.

Right:
Terry Lovett with crew from Rheinland Air Services on the initial Dusseldorf-EMA-Dusseldorf service which lasted less than four months - January 1995.

Above:
The Red Arrows BAe Hawk Display Team at East Midlands Airport – August 1992.

Left:
Her Majesty The Queen, pictured at East Midlands Airport in 1997, before heading off to Pride Park Stadium to officially open the new home of Derby County Football Club.

Right:
Following completion of this extension
work, the runway will be 2,893 metres
in length and provide airlines with the
opportunity to fly longer routes, using
quieter more modern aircraft.

Previous pages:
View from the tower towards
Donington Park Motor Racing Circuit
and ground work taking place for the
planned DHL hub – 1999.

Left:
Gulfstream's 40th anniversary Open Day
for Rolls Royce employees – 1998.

Right:
Groundwork on the Cargo West Apron,
with the DHL hub now nearing completion.

Previous pages:
United Parcel Service (UPS) established
East Midlands Airport as one of its key
European hubs - 1993.

Left:
The office element of the DHL building under construction.

Below Left:
The 300,000+ square foot DHL sorting facility takes shape.

Above:
A British Airways Concorde comes in to land watched by hundreds of enthusiasts at the Aeropark.

Right:
The number of Airlines and tour companies operating out of EMA is on the increase.

Far right:
Concorde rests between flights.

Mr Lovett said at the time: "This exciting project will provide 32 check-in desks and a departure baggage system that will cater for the Department of Transport's requirements for 100 per cent screening of hold baggage.

"Work is expected to commence on site in summer 1995 with the terminal being available to handle summer traffic in 1996."

While all this change was underway, it is not surprising that the airport's identity also fell under the spotlight.

When they purchased the airport in August 1993, National Express had agreed that they would not change the airport's name for at least 12 months.

But during 1994 extensive research was carried out and a list of more than 40 possible names for EMA were considered. These ranged from the obvious of Nottingham, Derby or Leicester, through location-based names such as Central England and Air Centre UK, to the more esoteric Robin Hood, Sherwood Forest or Ivanhoe.

The research suggested that if a change of name were to be made it should be to Nottingham; although it also demonstrated that there was no enthusiasm for the change amongst passengers, airlines or tour operators

In the end, a decision was made to remain as East Midlands Airport but to develop a new corporate identity, which was eventually launched in December 1994.

Back in 1991, Airport Chairman Peter Burgess had first raised the prospect of a high-quality business park on the airport site. However, it was not until March 1999 that work began on the 54-acre Pegasus Business Park, a joint venture between developers Wilson Bowden and EMA.

Spectacular progress followed, with the first completed building being a new regional headquarters for Powergen. This was followed by an Express by Holiday Inn hotel and a Regus office complex. The Pegasus Business Park is now an impressive feature of the NEMA site.

At the start of the decade EMA had produced a brochure entitled 'The Sky's The Limit' as part of a campaign designed to rebrand the airport's image and to demonstrate that the future was about meeting the needs of customers. The brochure was mailed out to decision-makers in more than 100 airlines.

When he left to take over as Managing Director at Manchester Airport, John Spooner said he went with the satisfaction of knowing that pretty much everything the airport required for the next 20 years was in place at EMA.

Following a decade of unprecedented investment and change Mr Spooner appeared to be right and, looking forward into the new millennium, the title of the marketing brochure seemed very apt.

Above:
With in excess of 6,500 people employed in and around the Airport site, demand for space on Pegasus Business Park is at a premium.

Chapter Five | 2000-2005

THE PAST FIVE years have seen a remarkable series of changes at Nottingham East Midlands Airport.

Use of the airport's new name highlights one change that continues to spark a fierce debate, but operational changes and new owners have perhaps been more fundamental in shifting people's perceptions of what the airport has to offer.

In 2000, the National Express Group decided that they wished to concentrate on their core transport business of buses, coaches and trains and, as a result, they put East Midlands Airport, and its sister airport Bournemouth International, up for sale.

March 2001 saw the Manchester Airport Group, which also included Humberside Airport, complete the purchase of East Midlands Airport and Bournemouth International Airport for £241 million. Eight years earlier National Express had paid just £24.3 million – a significant return on their investment.

Passenger figures in 2001 had seen an impressive seven percent rise to 2.38 million people, but a big change

was gathering pace that would result in passenger figures just three years later reaching 4.4 million people.

Low-cost air travel had arrived and East Midlands Airport now faced new challenges as this growing market captured the public's imagination.

Barry Thompson, Finance Director and Deputy Managing Director at Nottingham East Midlands Airport, says the low-cost airline boom has transformed the airport.

"The pace of change at Nottinghan East Midlands Airport has been remarkable in recent years.

"Before the low-cost market arrived, our scheduled flight programme was business-dominated. The general public was to some extent excluded because of the ticket prices.

"Then in spring 2002 we saw people coming down from Scotland to take advantage of low-cost flights out of NEMA.

"Quite simply, it put the airport on the map. It changed people's perception of the airport that, in turn, put us under new pressures. This has

always been a friendly and efficient airport; now we had a bigger audience to please.

"Everybody at the airport was determined to make it work. The challenge was to think differently. There was no blueprint to work to in relation to the low-cost market and this forced us to look at different methods of operation.

"We could not afford to play for a draw. To ensure that we succeeded, we had to stay close to our passengers and find out what they were looking for when they arrived at the airport."

Steve Gensler, who has worked at the airport since the early 1970s, has noted a change in the type of people who now pass through Nottingham East Midland Airport's terminal building.

Mr Gensler said: "Before low-cost we used to see predominantly package holiday and business types, but now we see a broader spectrum of people who perhaps do not have the loyalty to this airport that we have seen in the past."

Above:
Steve Gensler has seen many changes during the 33 years he has worked on the Airport site.

Opposite page:
Airside view of Nottingham East Midlands Airport.

Right:

TNT Airbus A300 freighter – July 2000.

Left:
Christmas 2000 and Santa Claus
arrives at EMA.

2000

**bmi launch new low-cost
airline at EMA – bmibaby**
March 2002

**GO announce EMA
as new base**
December 2001

**Manchester Airports
Group purchases EMA**
March 2001

**EMA gains ISO
14001 Environmental
Management
Standard**
October 2002

**Runway extension to
2,893m becomes fully
operational**
May 2000

**Graham Keddie
succeeds
John Spooner as
Airport Managing
Director**
November 2001

**New Aeropark opens
its gates**
August 2001

**DHL hub opens
at 'Cargo West'**
April 2000

2000

2001

George Bush elected US President

9/11 four US commercial airliners
hijacked by Islamic terrorists

2002

The Euro introduced in 11 of
the 15 EU member states

Queen's Golden Jubilee

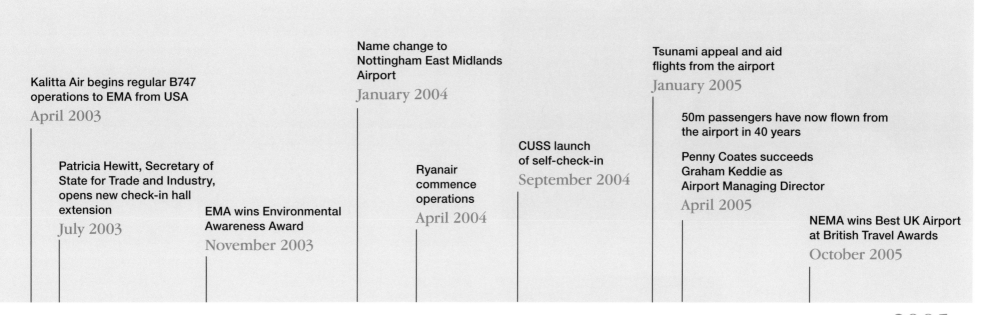

Name change to
Nottingham East Midlands
Airport
January 2004

Tsunami appeal and aid
flights from the airport
January 2005

Kalitta Air begins regular B747
operations to EMA from USA
April 2003

50m passengers have now flown from
the airport in 40 years

Patricia Hewitt, Secretary of
State for Trade and Industry,
opens new check-in hall
extension
July 2003

Ryanair
commence
operations
April 2004

CUSS launch
of self-check-in
September 2004

Penny Coates succeeds
Graham Keddie as
Airport Managing Director
April 2005

EMA wins Environmental
Awareness Award
November 2003

NEMA wins Best UK Airport
at British Travel Awards
October 2005

2005

2003

February
Space Shuttle Columbia disintegrates over Texas
upon re-entry, killing all seven astronauts

December
Saddam Hussein captured by US troops

2004

January
NASA's MER-A spacecraft lands on Mars

November
President George W Bush defeats Senator
John Kerry for a second term in office

2005

May
General Elections and Tony Blair wins
third successive term in Parliament

2005

Above:
Passengers queue for a GO flight
to Alicante.

Right:
Retail sales are a growing area of
the airport's business.

Human Resources Manager Dianne Letts echoed this view when she said: "We used to be known as a bucket and spade airport, but now low-cost has put the airport on the map with people looking for different experiences."

This new market opened up at East Midlands Airport with the announcement in December 2001 that low-cost airline GO was to operate flights out of the airport, which would become its third base in the UK.

Making the announcement, EMA Chairman Councillor Brian Harrison said: "In the past, thousands of passengers seeking low-cost services had been forced to drive past EMA's doors to reach other airports which were often located in the congested south east. We are sure that the benefit of these new plans will be two-fold; opening up new markets to travellers and offering more choice to our existing customers."

This was just the first shot in the low-cost battle that would dramatically drive up passenger numbers at the airport over the next few years.

In January 2002, just a month after the GO announcement, British Midland declared that it had chosen East Midlands as the base for its low-cost operation bmibaby.

By August 2001, GO and easyJet, who had recently merged, were announcing more routes from East Midlands Airport.

At the time, Barry Thompson said: "Today's move reflects a continuing demand for 'no-frills' travel from the region and we are pleased that our successful relationship with GO and easyJet allows us to offer our passengers greater travel choice."

The number of low-cost routes available from NEMA continues to grow. Ryanair commenced operations at the airport in April 2004, joining bmibaby and easyJet in offering low-cost services.

The low-cost airline market has evolved spectacularly during the last five years. In 2005 Ryanair, having become Europe's leading low-cost airline, confirmed that NEMA was to be one of its new bases.

Left:

The DHL hub - At the beginning of the decade Cargo West, a new £70 million complex funded jointly by NEMA and DHL Aviation, opened. At the heart of the Cargo West facility is a 350,000 square foot sorting facility, a 90,000 square foot three-storey office block, and a 120,000 square foot loading dock. Cargo West can accommodate 16 aircraft of varying size from Boeing 747s to Boeing 757s. The truck dock has room for 35 vehicles with remote spaces for a further 35. Along with bmi, DHL is now one of the biggest employers at NEMA.

Above:
Low-cost literally 'took off' in 2002 with Go/easyJet and bmibaby commencing operations.

Right:
John Baddiley, Airfield Engineering Supervisor, has seen many changes during his 29 years working for the airport.

From March 2006, the airline will base two brand new Boeing 737-800 aircraft, worth in excess of $120 million, at the Castle Donington site and, at the same time, will also increase its number of routes from five to 15.

Making the announcement Michael O'Leary, Chief Executive of Ryanair, said: "We are delighted to announce Nottingham East Midlands Airport as our 15th European base.

"From March 7th 2006, Ryanair will operate 15 routes through Nottingham East Midlands Airport delivering 1.2 million passengers per annum and therefore sustaining 1,200 jobs in the East Midlands area."

Another visible sign of the growth in passenger numbers driven by the low-cost market has been the extension to the airport's check-in hall.

But, while the focus has often fallen on the growing low-cost market, there has been another welcome development at Nottingham East Midlands Airport in 2005 with flights heading much further afield.

Both Britannia Airways in Summer 1992, and American Trans Air in Summer 1996 operated flights to Orlando. But it was a major step forward for NEMA when First Choice announced that it would be offering a long-haul programme from Nottingham East Midlands Airport in 2005.

Florida, Cancun in Mexico, and the Dominican Republic are now all available to holidaymakers jetting-out of the airport.

Perhaps the best way of demonstrating the dramatic growth in passenger numbers experienced in recent years is to highlight two recent milestones.

In November 2002, Mrs Tracy West of Heanor in Derbyshire was the 40 millionth passenger to pass through the airport terminal, 37 years after the start of operations in April 1965.

But just two-and-a-half years later in April 2005, a week after the airport had celebrated its official 40th birthday, Mrs Emma Barker from Alvaston in Derby became the 50 millionth passenger to use the airport.

Left:
Long haul passenger flights to the US returned when First Choice introduced holidays to Florida in 2005.

Following pages:
NEMA aerial photograph, produced by Infoterra - October 2003.

Right:
The check-in hall extension begins to
take shape. It was opened in early
July 2003 by the then Secretary of State
for Trade and Industry, Patricia Hewitt MP.

At a time when East Midlands Airport was experiencing unprecedented growth in its passenger numbers, Managing Director Graham Keddie revealed that EMA was working with the East Midlands Development Agency (emda) and a market research organisation to conduct a far-reaching survey aiming to find the most appropriate name for the airport.

On October 1st 2003, Mr Keddie said: "This research forms part of an ongoing commitment by the airport to continually assess the needs of its users and stakeholders as it experiences a period of sustained growth.

"It is running alongside long-term plans for the terminal and airport facilities to ensure expectations are not only met but exceeded.

"The effects of a name change on the region are very important to us at the airport, which is why we have decided to conduct the research."

The survey sought the opinions of the airport's major stakeholders, including local businesses, business organisations, development agencies, chambers of commerce, local authorities, city councils, members of parliament, the travel trade, tourism bodies, inbound and outbound passengers from both the business and leisure sectors, and people from local communities.

The survey was completed at the end of December 2003 and, on January 20th 2004, Mr Keddie announced that EMA would change its name to Nottingham East Midlands Airport.

Mr Keddie said: "We based the decision on purely commercial imperatives, taking into account the need to ensure the continued success of the airport and our airline partners at a time when increasing numbers of people are rightly choosing the more personal service and convenience of smaller regional airports over major international terminals.

"We believe that by doing this we are also serving our local UK passengers and the region in the best possible way."

Above:
This check-in hall extension, built adjacent to the airport's original check-in hall, cost £1.9 million and was necessary given that EMA was experiencing unprecedented growth in passenger numbers. The 3.2 million passengers recorded in 2002 represented a 36 percent increase on the previous year.

Left:
Graham Keddie, Managing Director from 2001-2005, said: "We look forward to a period of sustained growth whilst remaining committed to improving passenger facilities and maintaining our reputation as a friendly, easy to use airport."

Above:
An aerial photograph of the tower and main terminal buildings.

Right:
The pilots' view as they enter final approach to runway 09. Donington Park Motor Racing Circuit can be seen at the bottom of the picture.

"We are looking forward to seeing the new Nottingham East Midlands Airport become an even more popular departure and arrival location than it is today.

"Nottingham EMA makes commercial sense, not only for the airport, but for all of the major towns and attractions in the region. NEMA is looking forward to working with all local authorities to ensure that this opportunity is marketed to the full benefit of all."

The statement issued by the airport said that the decision addressed growing concerns that the airport's potential for growth was being inhibited by confusion in the minds of potential visitors from Europe and beyond about where exactly in the UK the East Midlands was located.

The survey had shown that Nottingham was the city within the region that had the most instant recognition and understanding overseas.

A major debate was to follow with many people claiming that the name

change was questionable.

Steve Gensler is among them. He said: "I believe the name change was a bad move. We immediately alienated some people. I would like to see a move back to a more inclusive name.

"The argument was that people on the Continent don't know where the East Midlands is. But the majority of traffic through this airport is UK-driven."

The debate continues. Some people are quite accepting of the name, others are not, and many just do not care what the airport is called so long as they get to where they are going in comfort and with no delay.

Seeking the views of people is a theme that runs through many of NEMA's activities these days. The airport is keen to engage in a dialogue with interested parties, particularly on issues that impact on the local environment.

NEMA's success in recent years, both in the passenger and cargo sectors, inevitably leads to more aircraft movements at the Castle Donington site.

Left:
Two Boeing 747s from Kalitta Air and Cathay Pacific Cargo airlines parked at Cargo West.

Right:
With well over 7000 car parking spaces on-site, the shuttle buses at the airport have a key role to play.

These days senior figures at the airport regularly engage with local people, their council representatives and local MPs to discuss the impact of the airport operations. Local surgeries in nearby villages and regular meetings with MPs are a feature of the airport's community relations.

Penny Coates, who was appointed Managing Director in 2005, said: "Our aim is to be a good neighbour.

"We want to ensure that quieter aircraft are used and we will make more information available to people – we have nothing to hide."

In October 2002, the airport had been the first in the UK to be certified to the ISO 14001 environment management standard.

The airport's desire to be a 'good neighbour' was formally recognised in November 2003 when it was named by the Environment Agency as the winner of the National Business Award for Environmental Awareness.

While presenting the Award, at a glittering ceremony at London's Grosvenor House Hotel, Sir John Harman, Chairman of the Environment Agency, made reference to a number of the airport's initiatives, including the monitoring of noise emissions and air quality. He also highlighted moves to adopt a systematic approach to controlling and minimising the impact of airport operations.

Sir John said: "We commend the efforts of East Midlands Airport to improve its environmental record.

"The environmental impact of aviation is considerable and the agency's position on aviation policy is on the record. But airports, in the way they are managed, can also have a significant impact on the environment and it is essential that environmental concerns are put at the heart of their business strategies. East Midlands Airport's entry proved to the judges that it has committed to doing so."

NEMA continues to take its responsibilities to the environment and local communities seriously and now provides a designated telephone number for people to use if they have concerns.

Above:
Sir John Harman (left) presents NEMA's Neil Robinson with the National Business Award for Environmental Awareness.

Left:
Penny Coates became the first female Managing Director of a UK airport when she was appointed to the role in April 2005.

Right:
A snowy view from the Air Traffic
Control Tower over the British Midland
engineering base and the DHL hub.

Left:
Another view from the tower following a heavy snowfall in January 2001. Ratcliffe-on-Soar Power Station can be seen in the distance.

Right:
DHL Air UK is based at NEMA and operates a fleet of 22 B757-200 special freighters on the DHL European overnight network. DHL, owned by Deutsche Post World Net, offer expertise in express, air and ocean freight.

The airport's Management Team are determined to ensure that major decisions are explained to as many affected people as possible. This was illustrated by the nature of the Airspace Consultation process that took place in the latter part of 2004 and into early 2005.

Following a statement in July 2004 welcoming a decision by the Civil Aviation Authority (CAA) to approve the airport's application to extend its controlled airspace, NEMA announced that it was seeking more time to consult with people affected by the move. The CAA supported this initiative, and issued a statement on August 27th 2004 agreeing to delay implementation of the new flight paths while further consultation took place.

John Froggatt, NEMA's Director of Planning and Development, said: "Although we have just completed a two year consultation, we owe it to our communities to listen to their concerns.

"It has been suggested that agreement to the new flight paths is effectively a green light for the uncontrolled growth of the airport. This is wrong.

"The airspace changes are required to enable us to control air traffic movements efficiently and to the highest safety standards. The growth of the airport is guided by Government policy and a rigorous planning process, which together ensure that major expansion proposals are subject to full scrutiny and individual approval."

In October 2004 the second period of consultation about changes to the airport's controlled airspace began, involving contact with some 200 local authorities and 700 individuals.

When this was completed, at the end of February 2005, NEMA was able to confirm that the CAA had approved their modified request for the additional airspace.

At that time, Mr Froggatt said: "We are confident that we have made every effort to listen to concerns in all our local communities, and have been able to allay many of the fears that were expressed. Where appropriate, we have made changes to our plans.

Above:
UPS has become an expert in global distribution which involves managing not only the movement of goods, but also the flow of information and finance that moves with those goods.

Right:
The continuing success of the Cargo West
facility, and of the activities of other cargo
operators based at NEMA, ensures that
today NEMA has a truly global reach.
In February 2003, the airport announced a
new long haul cargo operation by DHL and
Lufthansa Cargo with a five times a week
service to Hong Kong.

"Taken overall, the changes to controlled airspace will be of benefit to the community. Most aircraft will in future fly higher and more quietly than before, and low-level flying will be significantly reduced."

NEMA has launched other initiatives aimed at building partnerships with local communities too.

The Nottingham East Midlands Airport Community Fund supports projects within a 10-mile radius of NEMA. These projects can cover a wide variety of subjects, from environmental improvement to heritage conservation.

Since the Fund was launched in April 2002, £123,391 has been allocated to more than 180 projects.

Anna Thomson, from NEMA's Community Relations team, said: "In 2004, more than £40,000 worth of grants were pledged to more than 60 groups in the area.

"We take our commitment to being a good neighbour extremely seriously and the Fund is just one of the many initiatives that we have in place at the airport designed to give something back to the community."

However, one of the most contentious practices at NEMA will always be night flights by cargo aircraft.

At the beginning of the new decade a new complex opened, to be funded jointly by NEMA and DHL Aviation and known as Cargo West. The complex contains a 350,000 square foot sorting facility, a 90,000 square foot three-storey office block and a 120,000 square foot loading dock.

Cargo West can accommodate 16 aircraft of varying size, ranging from Boeing 747s to Boeing 757s.

The growth of NEMA as an air cargo hub has been spectacular, with freight flown through the airport rising from 179,135 tonnes in 2000 to 254,029 tonnes in 2004. Indications show that 2005 will see a further increase.

Mail flown from the airport during the same period has risen from 14,384 tonnes to 24,902 tonnes.

Announcing the 2004 results Bill Blanchard, NEMA's Cargo Development Manager, said:

"Nottingham East Midlands Airport has strengthened its position as the UK's number one 'pure cargo' airport and overtaken Gatwick to become the second largest cargo airport in the UK and the 13th largest in Europe.

"These figures show that companies are using NEMA more and more to ship their 'just in time' products by air. NEMA has always been a regional asset and now has a growing national role to play in this business.

"We are particularly pleased to see growth being achieved in an environmentally sustainable way. Compared to 2000, tonnage moved has grown by nearly 50 percent but has been carried on six percent fewer flights, using aircraft that are now much quieter, such as the B757."

As NEMA approached the close of its 40th-birthday year, a public opinion survey conducted by MORI seemed in some ways to endorse the vision of Eric Dyer and others who have worked so hard over four decades to make the airport the success it is today.

Above:

Bill Blanchard, Cargo Development Manager at NEMA, said: "We are particularly pleased to see growth being achieved in an environmentally sustainable way."

Above:
The new 3 Cities Bar opened this year in the extended and refurbished departure lounge.

Right:
NEMA directors Penny Coates and Barry Thompson present Mick Hodgkin (centre) with his 37 years long service award.

After conducting face-to-face interviews with more than 1,200 residents who live within a 12-mile radius of the airport and more than 300 people who live further than 25 miles away, results showed that 70 percent agreed that the airport was a good thing for the local area.

More than half the residents surveyed considered the impact of Nottingham East Midlands Airport to be a positive one and a clear majority said the airport brought economic benefits to the local area.

NEMA Managing Director Penny Coates said: "The results of the opinion poll demonstrate that there is much more support for NEMA than may be generally realised, particularly amongst those living closest to the airport.

"Nevertheless, we are not complacent about the need for us to do more to minimise the impact of our operations and to improve our communications with surrounding communities. The views contained in the survey will prove very useful in shaping future policies."

As October 2005 drew to a close NEMA also got the thumbs up at the British Travel Awards.

NEMA was nominated along with Gatwick, Manchester, Stansted and Birmingham airports in the 'Best UK Airport' category at the British Travel Awards 2005, and scooped the award at a ceremony in front of more than 2,500 senior members of the UK travel industry.

Caroline Plant, General Manager, Sales and Marketing at NEMA, is very proud of the airport's achievement: "We are absolutely delighted to have won the award for the Best UK Airport. The whole team here is thrilled and it shows how hard work and a great team spirit can overcome significant challenges in a tough competitive environment."

Maurice Boyle, Managing Director of Thomsonfly and part of the judging panel, said: "The panel's decision was reached after considering a number of criteria including ease of customer use, the airport's investment in new facilities and how easy it was to do business with from an airline and tour operator perspective.

"We recognised that NEMA had done a great job in each of these areas and is right up there with the more traditional heavyweight big hub airports."

So what of the boy seated at the top of Bardon Hill, what would he see if he turned his telescope towards the airport today?

Much the same, is the answer.

The airport complex from that distance would seem to have a similar profile, although there would be more aircraft movements to observe, more buildings scattered across the airport site, and more cars parked by those lucky enough to have jetted-off to some exotic destination.

Oh, and another thing, there would still be that same air of glamour.

Above:
The new executive lounge opened in 2005, part of the on-going development to improve facilities at NEMA.

Left and far left:
NEMA boasts an impressive array of shops and facilities.

Following pages:
The world's largest aircraft – the Antonov AN225 Myira – makes its first visit to NEMA on 28th November 2005. This was also the first commercial operation of the aircraft into the UK. A very fitting event during the airport's 40th anniversary year.

Epilogue

SO WHAT of the future?

The sustained growth in the popularity and success of NEMA with both members of the public and air cargo operators calls for an almost constant upgrading of the airport's facilities.

NEMA Managing Director Penny Coates was a regular user of the airport before assuming her current position. She enjoyed the airport's friendly welcome on many occasions and does not want to preside over a growth period that sees the airport becoming more impersonal.

Penny said: "In 2004 we recorded 4.4 million passengers and moved nearly 280,000 tonnes of cargo. Over the next decade, we can envisage more than doubling our passenger numbers and an even higher rate of growth in our cargo volumes. Our projections represent a huge challenge to all of us at the airport.

"Soon we will be seeking planning permission for a major extension to the terminal building that we are hoping to see completed by 2008/9. It is my intention that this will change only the face of NEMA, not the personality.

"People enjoy the convenience of using a local airport. But convenience is not enough: we must provide our customers with the experience they are looking for, each and every time they come to NEMA.

"We care about our passengers and we are determined to keep the same friendly atmosphere that has existed here for so long. We must succeed in meeting our growth projections with the unique character of the airport still in place. Our aim is always to enhance our visitors' overall experience, by improving the facilities available and by increasing the number and variety of our destinations, especially on the long-haul routes.

"But, as we move forward, we must also look beyond our own immediate boundaries. We want to work together with other organisations to promote the East Midlands as a whole, so that we can bring benefits to everyone here.

"The number of overseas visitors using NEMA as their point of entry to the UK is already growing strongly, and we will be well positioned in 2012 to ensure that visitors planning to attend the London Olympics are made aware of the additional attractions the East Midlands has to offer as well.

"But our growth is not just about passenger numbers and cargo volumes: we are an integral part of the regional economy and, in years to come, we can expect to see perhaps 20,000 to 30,000 people employed in and around the airport site. Employment opportunities for Derby, Leicester, Nottingham and the surrounding areas will be substantial. Furthermore, we can anticipate associated benefits from an enhanced public transport system in and out of the airport.

"Over the last 40 years, NEMA has become a terrific regional success story. We can be justifiably proud of what has been achieved. But there is always room for improvement and we must be prepared to learn lessons from the past.

Opposite page:
NEMA Directors (left to right): John Froggatt, Barry Thompson and Penny Coates realise there are major challenges ahead if the airport is to keep pace with the increased demand for air travel.

Right:
An artist's impression of how the extended terminal may look in the future.

"As we look forward, I am committed to a policy of clear and open communication about our aspirations, so that the people affected by our operations will be better able to contribute to our plans and help to shape our collective future.

"As with so many things, the secret is to get the balance right. We must weigh carefully the pros and cons of our alternative options whilst recognising both the importance of our role in the local economy and the impact we have on the amenity of our surrounding environment. And when the way forward is clear, we must act decisively and efficiently to make the most of our opportunities.

"I have no doubt that there is an exciting future ahead for all of us."

Above:
NEMA staff celebrate at The British Travel Awards 2005 having been voted 'Best UK Airport'.
Back row (from left to right): Debbie Malone, Caroline Plant, Jessica Dear, Sarah Fletcher, and Brooke Boger. Ryan Martinez holds the award.

Finale:
NEMA celebrates its 40th anniversary with
a variety of events throughout 2005.
Scenes from a spectacular summer ball
aptly titled 'The Ruby Do' in the grounds
of Kedleston Hall in Derby, a luncheon
for the Airport's Retirement Association
and a birthday party for passengers in the
check-in hall.